OUTLINE

OF A

COURSE OF ENGLISH READING,

BASED ON THAT PREPARED FOR THE MERCANTILE LIBRARY ASSOCIATION OF THE CITY OF NEW-YORK, BY THE LATE CHANCELLOR KENT, WITH ADDITIONS BY CHAS. KING, LL.D., PRESIDENT OF COLUMBIA COLLEGE, NEW-YORK.

EDITED, WITH FURTHER ADDITIONS AND NOTES,

BY

HENRY A. OAKLEY.

NEW-YORK:
G. P. PUTNAM AND CO., 10 PARK PLACE.
1853.

JOHN F. TROW, PRINTER,
49 Ann-Street.

PREFACE.

THIS work is based upon a course of English Reading prepared in 1840 for the use of the members of the Mercantile Library Association of this city, by the late Chancellor Kent, which has for many years been entirely out of print. The numerous inquiries that were made for the work, led the Board of Directors for 1851, to place the original book in the hands of Charles King, Esq., President of Columbia College, for the purpose of enlargement.

After such enlargement, however, it was found that the work could be materially improved, and its value much enhanced, by adopting another mode of arrangement, and by making further additions to it, and the undersigned was requested to undertake its preparation. He did so with a full sense of the difficulty of preparing a course of reading upon almost every branch of English literature, that should be both useful to the student and practical in its tendency, and, as a matter of course, has been obliged to confine himself mostly to general heads. It is not presumed that the work is at all perfect—it is defective in many particulars, but still it will serve as a guide for the class for whom it was especially designed, and, it is also hoped, for others, in pursuing various branches of study. And in order further to facilitate the student, those works which are deemed to be the most important ones to be read upon any of the various subjects, and whose perusal will give the reader a good general idea of his subject, are designated by the figure (1), and those which illustrate any of the subjects more particularly, by the figure (2). Such students as may wish to investigate thoroughly any of the various branches of study, are further recommended to those designated by the figure (3), and to the other works not numbered. It will be found that upon most of the branches of study, or periods mentioned, a full and sufficient knowledge can be obtained. The whole of the works recommended by Chancellor Kent have been retained, though, in many instances, they have been superseded by more recent and more valuable works. Care has been taken also, to give due credit, as far as was practicable, to the suggesters of the works that have been added ; and it is hoped that the success of the present issue will be an inducement to undertake a work, which shall be more full in its details, and otherwise a truly valuable guide to the student of English literature.

HENRY A. OAKLEY.

NEW-YORK, November, 1852.

CONTENTS.

I. HISTORY.

	PAGE
General,	1
Ancient Mythology,	3
Greece,	3
Rome,	6
Palestine,	10
Egypt,	10
Other Ancient Nations,	11

II. MODERN HISTORY.

Europe Generally,	12
Italy,	14
Germany, Austria, and Hungary,	16
France—Generally,	17
" The Revolution and Empire,	19
England Generally,	21
" Special Portions of English History,	23
Scotland,	25
Ireland,	26

PAGE
Spain and Portugal, ... 26
Switzerland, ... 28
Turkey and Greece, ... 28
Russia and Poland, ... 28
Holland, Denmark, Sweden, and Norway, . . . 29
Asiatic and African Powers, ... 30
America Generally, ... 32
The United States, ... 32
War of Independence, ... 37
War of 1812, ... 39
The Mexican War, ... 40
Other Parts of America, ... 41

III. BIOGRAPHY.

Biographical Dictionaries, ... 43
American, ... 43
European, ... 47

IV. TRAVELS.

United States, ... 53
Other Parts of America, ... 57
Europe Generally, ... 59
Great Britain, ... 60
France, ... 61
Spain and Portugal, ... 62
Italy and Sicily, ... 63
Holland, Belgium, and Central Europe, ... 64
North of Europe, ... 66
Western Asia, ... 67
Eastern Asia, and the Pacific Islands, ... 70
Africa, ... 72

V. VOYAGES.

PAGE
Southern Hemisphere, and Pacific, ... 75
Northern Seas, ... 78

VI. BELLES-LETTRES—ANCIENT.

Greek Oratory, Philosophy, and Poetry, . . . 80
Roman Oratory, Philosophy, and Poetry, ... 82

VII. BELLES-LETTRES—MODERN.

General Literature, ... 85
Essays, Criticisms, Literary History, ... 87
Poetry, ... 93
Drama, ... 100
Arts, ... 102
Prose Fiction, ... 103
American Works of Fiction, ... 107

VIII. GAMES, SPORTS, AND AMUSEMENTS.

Games, Sports, and Amusements, ... 109

IX. POLITICAL SCIENCE.

Constitutional and Commercial Law, ... 109

X. MORAL SCIENCE.

Moral Science, ... 112

XI. NATURAL SCIENCES.

PAGE

Natural Philosophy, Chemistry, Geology, Mineralogy, &c., . . 115
Natural History, ... 118
Astronomy, ... 119
Botany, ... 120

COURSE OF READING.

I.

ANCIENT HISTORY.

I. GENERAL.

1. Ancient Writers.

Herodotus.

Translated by William Beloe.

Every investigation made by travellers and geographers in modern times, has tended to confirm the good faith, truth, and accuracy of Herodotus, who is styled the "Father of History."—*Kent.*

Herodotus.

Translated by Henry Cary.

More condensed than Beloe's translation, and esteemed by many preferable on that account.

Polybius' "General History."

Translated by Hampton.

It is a history of the Greek and Roman world during the most splendid march of the Roman power from the beginning of the Second Punic War to the end of the kingdom of Macedon. The history is interwoven with sound political reflections.—*Kent.*

2. Modern Writers.

Rollin's Ancient History (2).

Written in French, and translated.

This has been a standard work in the Schools for a century past in relation to Egyptian, Assyrian, Carthaginian, and Grecian history; and it is a popular compilation of surpassing excellence.—*Kent.*

Muller, K. O. History and Antiquities of the Doric Race (2). From the German.—*Ch. King.*

Heeren on the Ancient Nations of Africa, &c. (1).

1. The Carthaginians, Egyptians, and Ethiopians. 2 vols.
2. The Asiatic Nations. 2 vols.
3. Sketch of the Political History of Ancient Greece. 1 vol.
4. Manual of Ancient History. 1 vol.

These works are all translated from the German; they are deeply instructive, and replete with striking and sagacious reflections.—*Kent.*

Niebuhr's Lectures on Ancient History (1).

3 vols.

Taylor's Manual of Ancient History (1).

Comprehensive and carefully prepared.

Tytler's Elements of General History, Ancient and Modern (1).

Well worth consulting.

3. Chronological Tables.

Blair. Chronological and Historical Tables.

Revised by Sir Henry Ellis. Small folio. London, 1844.

"*The Oxford Chronological Tables.*"

Folio. (Now published in London.)

These very full and comprehensive tables were prepared by the late D. A. Talboys, the publisher, of Oxford, who also translated several of Heeren's works.

Putnam. The World's Progress.

12mo. New-York.

Contains concise tables of ancient and modern chronology.

Nicolas, Sir H. Chronology of History.

Containing Tables, &c. 8vo. London, 1840.

4. Ancient Mythology.

Smith, William. Dictionary of Greek and Roman Biography and Mythology (2). 3 vols. 8vo. London.

Smith, William. Dictionary of Greek and Roman Antiquities (2). Edited by Prof. Charles Anthon.

This work may be deemed indispensable to the student of ancient history and literature, and is of great use to the general reader.—*Ch. King.*

Lemprière, John. Classical Dictionary (2).
Edited and much enlarged by Prof. Anthon.

Keightley, Thomas. Mythology of Ancient Greece and Italy (1).

Dwight, M. A. Grecian and Roman Mythology (1).

An elegant summary, prepared by a lady.

Christmas, Rev. H. Universal Mythology (3).

II. GREECE.

1. Ancient Writers.

Herodotus. (See page 1.)

Thucydides.

Translated by William Smith.

His work was devoted to the memorable Peleponnesian War between Athens and Sparta. He was one of the most eminent of the ancient historians, and a model of simplicity, conciseness, and scrupulous fidelity.—*Kent.*

Another translation. By Rev. Dr. S. T. Bloomfield.

Is "valuable for its notes."

Xenophon—his History of the Affairs of Greece.

Translated by William Smith, the translator of Thucydides. It takes up the narrative where Thucydides leaves off.

His Expedition of Cyrus and Retreat of the Ten Thousand was admirably translated by Spelman, and it is a fascinating narration to all admirers of Grecian enterprise and discipline.

His institution of Cyrus, called Cyrodœpia, translated by Ashley, has rather been considered a philosophical romance than an authentic history. It, however, details the conduct of a wise and virtuous king.—*Kent.*

Plutarch's Lives (1).

Translated by the two LANGHORNES from the original Greek.

Plutarch has for ages been the most popular of all the ancient historical writers.—*Kent.*

⁂ The above comprise the leading original Greek historians.

2. MODERN WRITERS.

Grecian history has been illustrated and adorned in a more especial manner by modern authors, and the following are recommended as being the most worthy of confidence and study:—

Goldsmith, Oliver. History of Greece (2).

A delightful summary, for Dr. Johnson's epitaph on Goldsmith says truly, that his pen touched no subject he did not adorn.—*Kent.*

It is more generally esteemed to be uncritical, and wanting in accuracy.

Gillie's History of Greece (2),

And his *History of the World*, from Alexander to Augustus,

Are works which show that the author was profoundly versed in Grecian learning and antiquities.—*Kent.*

Barthelmy, Abbé. The Travels of Anacharsis (2).

This work has been highly extolled, and greatly admired as a rich mine of Grecian erudition and elegant literature. It is a very learned and ingenious view of the Greek institutions, arts, and manners, in the form of a fictitious voyage, by a young Scythian, into Greece in the midst of her glory. —*Kent.*

Mitford's History of Greece (3).

This great work is distinguished for its accuracy, freedom, and trustworthiness. He does not scruple to tell the truth, and the whole truth, and to paint the stormy democracies of Greece in all their grandeur, and in all their wretchedness.—*Kent.*

Mitford is censured by Thirlwall and others as displaying too much of a partisan spirit.

Muller, K. O. History and Antiquities of the Doric Race. (See page 2.)

Wacksmuth. Historical Antiquities of the Greeks.
Translated from the German, by EDWARD WOOLRYCH.—*King.*

Heeren's Ancient Greece (2).
From the German, by GEORGE BANCROFT.

Few writers have better succeeded in treating questions of antiquity with the spirit of modern philosophical criticism.—*North Am. Rev.*

Grote's History of Greece (1).
10 vols. 8vo. Lond. Reprinted, 10 vols. 12mo.; Boston.

The work of an original thinker, and a true lover of liberty.—*Ch. King.*

Thirlwall. History of Greece (1).

Although the author's fancy is every where subject to his correct historical taste, the student will not fail to detect traces of that scholar-like delight in the graceful and lovely fictions of antiquity, which is so peculiarly attractive to minds of congenial temper. It animates the reader through the toilsome intricacy of some parts of his progress, like a brook by the way-side, which though it only sparkles in the traveller's eye, yet enlivens him by the sense of its constant companionship—*Edin. Rev.*

Smith's Dictionary of Greek and Roman Biography (1).
(See p. 3.)

Smith, William. Dictionary of Greek and Roman Antiquities (2). (See p. 3.)

New-York Review.

Nos. 13 and 17, for two able and scholarly papers, by the late Hugh Swinton Legare, of South Carolina—one on the Constitutional History of Greece, the other on Demosthenes,—eminently worthy of study.—*Ch. King.*

Schmitz's History of Greece (1).
12mo.

Concise, clear, and accurate.

Keightley's History of Greece (1).
12mo.

St. John's History of the Manners, Customs, &c., of Ancient Greece (2). 3 vols. 8vo.

Very learned and judicious.

Wordsworth's Classical Tour in Attica, &c. (2). 8vo.

Browne's History of Greek Classical Literature (1). 8vo.

III. ROME.

1. Ancient Writers.

Sallust's Histories of Catiline's Conspiracy (2), *and of the War with Jugurtha.* Translated by Rose and Stewart.

Are masterly productions, written with wonderful conciseness and energy, and with sketches of character and of picturesque incidents, that are inimitable.—*Kent.*

Dionysius of Halicarnassus (3).

Flourished in the Augustan age. His Roman Antiquities relate to the early history of Rome, down to the first Punic War. They are translated by the learned Spelman.—*Kent.*

Livy (2).

Translated by Baker.

This history is upon the whole the greatest and most comprehensive historical composition of the ancients. It is replete with gravity, sincerity, and picturesque description. The third decade on the Invasion of Italy by Hannibal, is the grandest exhibition of power and talent, to be met with in story. The translation is simple and dry, but true and exact.—*Kent.*

Julius Cæsar's Wars in Gaul (1).

Translated by Duncan.

The history is written with great simplicity and candor.—*Kent.*

Tacitus (1).

Translated by Murphy.

All the remains of Tacitus are deserving of profound study. The translation wants the compression of the original, and is too periphrastic. The English language would not well admit of the brevity of Tacitus, without rendering the narration abrupt and obscure. The translation is distinguished for elegance and strength, and dignity, and gives the sense of the original with fidelity.—*Kent.*

Plutarch's Lives (1). (See p. 4.

2. Modern Writers.

Among the many writers of modern times upon Roman History, it will be sufficient to mention

Hooke's Roman History (3).

From the foundation of Rome to the ruin of the Commonwealth.

This occupies the whole ground that Livy had chosen. He was a laborious and faithful compiler. The Jesuits, Catrou and Rouillé, far exceeded him, for they compiled a Roman History in 21 vols. 4to., and which is the most extensive Roman History extant.—*Kent.*

Rollin's History of Rome (2).

With Crevier's History of the Roman Emperors.

Is of high character for fidelity, but it is very prolix and tediously minute. I entered upon the reading of a translation of it when at College sixty years ago, with inconsiderate ardor, but was soon glad to escape to Goldsmith's brief and enchanting epitome of Roman History.—*Kent.*

Niebuhr's History of Rome (1).

Translated from the German by Hare and Thirlwall.

It calls in question the authority of much of the early Roman history; and the author is a searching and profound antiquary. The first centuries of the Roman Republic are intermixed, no doubt, with much beautiful fiction created by national vanity, and at the same time with much solid truth. The work has too much of dry and intricate antiquarian research and criticism, to interest the general reader.—*Kent.*

Vertot's Revolutions of Rome (3).

The narration is beautiful and eloquent.—*Kent.*

Ferguson's History of the Progress and Termination of the Roman Republic (2).

Authentic and dignified; and the latter volumes, on the struggles and termination of the Republic, are full of interesting reflection.—*Kent.*

Goldsmith's History of Rome, from its Foundation to the Destruction of the Western Empire (2).

A delightful summary. See respecting the Author's History of Greece. —*Kent.*

Montesquieu on the Grandeur and Declension of the Romans (3).

Greatly admired; and D'Alembert called it a Roman History, for the use of statesmen and philosophers.—*Kent.*

Middleton's Life of Cicero (3).

May be considered as a most important branch of Roman history. It is an admirable work. The life of that great man spreads over the whole interesting period of the dying convulsions of the Republic.—*Kent.*

Gibbon's History of the Decline and Fall of the Roman Empire (2). With notes by H. H. MILMAN and GUIZOT.

Some of the notes disfigure the work, and are in bad taste; but the work itself is a great, splendid, and perhaps unrivalled monument of talent, industry and learning. Milman's notes are a valuable corrective.—*Kent.*

Sismondi's History of the Fall of the Roman Empire (2). —*Kent.*

Arnold. History of Rome (1).

——— *Later Roman Commonwealth* (1).

Works full of value, and written in a clear perspicuous style, by an original thinker and learned man.

Knight, Charles. Social Life of the Romans (2).

Eliot, Samuel. Liberty of Rome, and Ancient Nations (2).

The character of this remarkable American work, may be in part surmised from one of the mottoes on its title-page. "The history of the World is one of God's own great poems." Its aim in tracing accurately and philosophically the struggles of Rome after liberty, is to show, that over antiquity as over our own times, an overruling Providence prevailed, and that none can fathom the truths of history but with the plummet of Revelation. It maintains, and satisfactorily elucidates the great truth of the universality of the Divine government, as the groundwork of every history that deserves the name.—*Ch. King.*

Lynam. History of the Roman Emperors (2).

D'Arnay. Private Life of the Romans (2).

Gell, Sir Wm. Topography of Rome (1).

Anthon, Charles. A Manual of Roman Antiquities (1).

Mahon, Lord. Life of Belisarius (2).

This story will never lose its interest, nor its moral of the instability of human grandeur, and Mahon adheres to the old version of it, in spite of Gibbon and more recent writers.—*Ch. King.*

Ware, William. Probus, or Rome in the Third Century (2). 2 vols.

—— —— *Zenobia, or the Fall of Palmyra* (2). 2 vols.

Works which have gained for their author a brilliant reputation as an elegant writer, and accomplished scholar.

Smith, William. Dictionary of Greek and Roman Biography (1). (See p. 3.)

Smith, William. Dictionary of Greek and Roman Antiquities (2). (See p. 3.)

Schmitz's History of Rome (1).
12mo. Valuable and reliable.

Keightley's History of Rome (1).
12mo.

Plutarch's Civil Wars of Rome.
Translated by Professor C. Long. 5 vols. 18mo.

Browne's History of Roman Literature (1).
8vo.

Eustace's Classical Tour through Italy in 1802.

IV. PALESTINE—THE JEWS.

1. Ancient Writers.

The Historical Parts of the Old Testament.

Josephus: Jewish Antiquities.
Translated by Whiston. The same by Traill.

☞ The death of the Author has left this valuable translation incomplete.

2. Modern Writers.

Prideaux: Connection between the Old and New Testaments (1).

Shuckford's Sacred and Profane History of the World Connected (2).

Lewis' Antiquities of the Hebrew Republic (1).

Milman's History of the Jews (2).
To be read with caution.

Turner's Sacred History of the World.

Jenning's Jewish Antiquities (1).

Kitto's History of Palestine and the Jews (1).

Burder's Oriental Customs and Literature (2.)

Smith's Hebrew People.

Gleig's History of Bible (2).

V. EGYPT.

1. Ancient Writers.

Herodotus. (See p. 1.)

2. Modern Writers.

Wilkinson, J. G. The Manners and Customs of the Ancient Egyptians.

Including their Private Life, Government, Laws, Charts, Manufactures, Religion, and Early History. An instructive as well as interesting work, not entirely original, but reliable and authentic.

Russell. History of Egypt (1).

A condensed History of Ancient and Modern Egypt.

Sharpe, Edward. Egypt under the Ptolemies (2).

——— ——— *Egypt under the Romans* (2).

Kenrick. Egypt under the Pharaohs (1).
2 vols.

Hawks, Rev. Dr. The Monuments of Egypt; or, Egypt a Witness for the Bible (1). 8vo.

Hengstenberg. Egypt and Books of Moses (1).

Bunsen. Egypt's Place in Universal History.
8vo.

Osburn. Antiquities of Egypt (1).

6. Other Ancient Nations.

Rollin's Ancient History. (See p. 1.)

Heeren on the Ancient Nations of Africa, etc. (See p. 2.)

Russell, Michael. History of the Barbary States.

A succinct outline of these remarkable provinces, under the dominion of the Phœnicians, Romans, Vandals, &c., &c.

Niebuhr's Lectures on Ancient History. 3 vols.

Taylor's Manual of Ancient History (1). (See p. 2.)

II.

MODERN HISTORY.

I. EUROPEAN, GENERALLY.

Gibbon.—Decline and Fall of the Roman Empire.

With Notes, by Rev. H. H. Millman and Guizot. (See page 8.)

Russell.—History of Modern Europe (2).

Tytler's and Nare's Universal History (2).

These compilations will give a general view of history, and may serve for such persons as have not leisure to consult and read higher authorities, or enter into more accurate details.—*Kent.*

Taylor's Manual of Modern History (1).

Concise but valuable.

Voltaire's Essay upon the Manners and Spirit of Nations.

And the principal facts of history, from Charlemagne to Louis 13th.

This is an elaborate work; and in the earlier editions of Voltaire's works, it was entitled an "Essay on General History." Gibbon says that Voltaire "cast a keen and rapid glance over the surface of history." Nothing could be more just and graphic than this character of Voltaire's history. It is nevertheless written with great vivacity, beauty, sagacity and taste. His "Age of Louis 14th" is the most celebrated, and the most admired of all his historical productions.—*Kent.*

James's History of Charlemagne (1).

Is an admirable work.—*Kent.*

Vertot's History of the Knights of Malta.

It is a very spirited, elegant, and interesting work; but Gibbon cast a shade over its accuracy, in saying that the Abbé had a turn for romance, and wrote to please the order.—*Kent.*

Ranke's History of the Popes (1).

Translated by Foster. Also by Mrs. Austin. From the German.

To be read by all who would judge for themselves of the mysterious power and boundless pretension of the papacy.—*Ch. King.*

Heeren, A. H. L.—Political System of Europe (2).

Mills.—History of Chivalry.

——— *History of the Crusades.*

Very interesting and full of valuable information.

Father Paul's History of the Council of Trent (3).

Translated by Brent, London, 1620, with a fulsome dedication to King James.

The Council of Trent was called by the Pope in 1536; but it did not formally assemble until 1545. It was a great event in ecclesiastical history, and was called for the avowed purpose of "cleansing the church from heresy, restoring discipline, correcting manners, and making war against infidels." Father Paul's history is very celebrated; and Dr. Robertson places it among the most admired historical compositions, for perspicuity, erudition, and force of reason. The historian himself was one of the most amiable, elevated and patriotic characters that was ever formed in monastic retirement. —*Kent.*

Burnet's History of the Reformation (1).

By Dr. Nares.

He wrote with coarseness, vigor, and integrity.—*Kent.*

Bishop Burnet's work is generally recognized as a standard. The author's Abridgment is very good for general use.

D'Aubigné's History of the Reformation (2).

One sided, but full of matter.—*Ch. King.*

Mosheim's Ecclesiastical History (1).

Translated from the German, by Maclaine, and recently by Murdock.

An excellent work. He has been called the Father of Ecclesiastical History.—*Kent.*

Maclaine's version is not reliable.

Gieseler's Ecclesiastical History (1).

3 volumes.

Very valuable for its notes and citations from original authorities.

Alison's History of Europe (1).

From the Commencement of the French Revolution.

It is one of the most authentic and most eloquent historical productions of the age.—*Kent.*

Miller, Samuel. Retrospect of the Eighteenth Century (2).

Schlegel's Lectures on Modern History (2).

Translated from the German.

Smyth, William. Lectures on Modern History (1).

Edited by JARED SPARKS.

These lectures will enable students and readers generally to read history for themselves, to show them the path and furnish them with the best means of pursuing it, and enable them to form a just estimate of the principal authors, and to bring forward in bold relief those prominent parts of history to which their attention should be chiefly directed.—*Jared Sparks.*

Arnold. Lectures on the Study of Modern History (1).

Dr. Arnold acquaints his readers with the nature and value of the treasure for which they are searching, and this he does with a perspicuity, simplicity and beauty of language, and a strength and originality of thought, that shows him to have possessed both the art and the power of the finished historian.—*J. G. Cogswell.*

Hallam's History of Europe During the Middle Ages (1).

Maitland's Dark Ages (2).

II. ITALY.

Machiavelli's History of the Republic of Florence (3).

Was written at the request of Pope Clement 7th, and is carried down to the death of Lorenzo de Medici. He was the Florentine Secretary of State, and eminent for his political sagacity and profound depth of observation. The first book is deemed a model of historical abridgment of the history of the former sovereignties of Italy. He has been hailed as the Morning Star of modern history; and in reference to his strong and stern remark, and lively and picturesque description, he has been styled the Tuscan Tacitus. His history is very instructive and monitory, inasmuch as it describes the ferocity of faction, and civil dissension incident to the popular and stormy democracies of ancient Greece and modern Italy, and the proscriptions and tyranny in which they all eventually terminated.—*Kent.*

Guicciardini's History of the Civil Wars in Italy (3).

He begins where Machiavel ended his history of Florence; and it consequently embraced the last struggles of the republic of Florence. He was a severe and impartial historian, and took a deep share in the civil and military affairs of Italy; but his history is painfully prolix and attenuated. It is entitled "The History of Italy from 1490 to 1532," and was translated into English by Goddard, in the middle of the last century. The history of Guicciardini has been uniformly admired for its exactness and veracity, and Sir William Jones went so far as to say, that he believed it was the most authentic history that was ever composed. But he gives a most deplorable picture of Italian society and morals in the 15th and 16th centuries. His pictures of the worst vices of Italy resemble those sketches in the great Greek historian; and he has frequently been called the Florentine Thucydides.—*Kent.*

Roscoe's Lives of Lorenzo de Medici, and of Leo 10th (1).

Have been greatly celebrated, for they give a learned and elegant history of civil affairs and of letters in Italy during the time that Lorenzo governed the Florentine republic and throughout "Leo's golden days." The first of these works, which appeared in 1795, as the production "of a practising attorney, to use the words of a critic of that day, in the remote commercial town of Liverpool, where nothing was heard of but Guinea ships, blacks, and merchandise," struck the men of letters in London with surprise and admiration, as a phenomenon in Literature. The history received in consequence extravagant praise, and was placed in the first rank of English classical history. But the progress of time, and higher attainments in criticism, have contributed to abate much of this original enthusiasm. The life of Leo 10th is dull and tedious, and both histories have now attained a stationary but moderate elevation.—*Kent.*

The best edition of these works is the Lond. Edit. of 1849, in 4 vols. 8vo.

Gianonne's Civil History of the Kingdom of Naples,

In 11 volumes,

Is much esteemed. Lord Mansfield recommended it to the student. It is distinguished for purity of style, and for freedom and boldness of discussion; and the severity with which he treated the church, exposed him to terrible persecution, exile and imprisonment.—*Kent.*

Sismondi's History of the Italian Republics of the Middle Ages (1).

He afterwards abridged it under the title of a View of the Origin, Progress, and Fall of Italian Freedom.—*Kent.*

Procter's History of Italy (2).

Ranke's History of the Popes (1). (See p. 12).

Smedley, E. Sketches from Venetian History (2).

Adams (Pres.) John. Defence of the American Constitution.

The 2d and 3d volumes give an abridgment of the histories of the Italian republics of the middle ages, between the fall of the Western and the Eastern Empires. He refers to the histories of the republics of Florence, Sienna, Bologna, Pistoria, Cremona and Padua; and his object was to demonstrate, (as he did effectually) the imperfections of their political systems, and that they were all alike ill-constituted; all alike miserable; and all ended in similar disgrace and despotism.—*Kent.*

Napier, H. F. Florentine History (1).

III. GERMANY, AUSTRIA, HUNGARY.

Coxe. History of the House of Austria (2).

Robertson. History of the Reign of the Emperor Charles V. (1).

Sterling productions, of the highest order.

Menzell. History of Germany (3).

Valuable for its descriptive merit, though not remarkable for deep research.

Schiller's History of the Thirty Years' War (1).

Ranke's History of the House of Brandenburgh.
Translated from the German, by Sir A. GORDON.

Kohlrausch, Fred. History of Germany (1).

Dover, Lord. Life of Frederick the Great.

Russell. History of Modern Europe. (See page 12.)

Bougeant's History of the Wars and Negotiations which preceded the Treaty of Westphalia.

The first volume is devoted to the famous Thirty Years' War in Germany, and it is animated and deeply attractive.—*Kent.*

Pardoe, Miss. City of the Magyars (2).

A valuable work, full of information relative to this most interesting people.

Paget, John. Hungary and Transylvania.

Pulsky, Theresa. Memoirs of a Hungarian Lady (2).
With a Historical Introduction, by Francis Pulsky.

Schlesinger's Hungary.

Pragay, Col. J. Outline of the Leading Events attending the Hungarian Struggle for Freedom (2).

Klapka, Gen. War of Independence in Hungary (2).

Tefft, Rev. B. F., D. D. Hungary and Kossuth (2).

These volumes will give the reader a lucid and full narrative of the Hungarian War. The first two were written by participators in the struggle, whose opportunities of information render their accounts reliable. The last work is the production of an American, well and dispassionately written.

IV. FRANCE.

Davila's History of the Civil Wars in France (3).

Was written originally in Italian, at Venice, and treats of the civil wars of France from 1559 to 1598. The French, who are the best judges in the case, praise the work for the historian's happy power of narration, the striking verity and vivacity of his descriptions, and his sagacious investigation of the springs of action in princes and statesmen.—*Kent.*

Sismondi's History of France, 31 *vols.* (3).

He narrates freely, and with his usual spirit and eloquence.—*Kent.*

Michelet, J. History of France (2).

The productions of one of the most learned and eloquent of the living historians of France; and in such historians no country is so rich.—*Bp. Potter.*

Crowe. History of France (2).

Smedley's History of France (1).

Pardoe, Miss. Louis XIV. and the Court of France (2).

——— ——— *Francis I., his Court and Reign* (2).

"Charming narratives."

History of Louis XI., by Duclos (3).

It relates to an interesting age, and to a faithless and rapacious, but sagacious and vigorous despot, who worked a revolution in the government of France. His character must be familiar to the English reader; for who has not read his portrait in Quentin Durward, as drawn by the masterly pencil of Scott?—*Kent.*

De Retz's Memoirs (2).

Are light, graceful, amusing, full of incident, and in keeping with the French character of that day.—*Kent.*

Sully's Memoirs (2).

They are very interesting, and place the character of Sully in an amiable light, as an honest and able statesmen. Hume says, that Henry IV., who figures so largely in these memoirs, was the most heroic and most amiable prince that adorns modern story.—*Kent.*

Thierry's Merovingian Era (2).

James's Life of Henry IV. (1).

France—The Revolution and the Empire.

Mignet's History of the French Revolution (2).

Thiers. History of the French Revolution (1).

Carlyle. History of the French Revolution (2).

To be read in connection, and thus with profit. Thiers seems too much the apologist of the excesses of the revolution, but is a faithful chronicler of its incidents, with his details full in the mind. The picture gallery of Carlyle, in which men and events are grouped, in a way that leaves indelible impressions and becomes a great study.—*Ch. King.*

Abbott. Life of Marie Antoinette (1).

An appreciative narrative of the life of this lovely but unfortunate lady.

Lamartine. History of the Girondists (2).

An eloquent and glowing memorial of the brilliant, but visionary and inexperienced deputies of the Gironde, who vainly hoped to guide the whirlwind of revolution which they were instrumental in exciting.—*Ch. King.*

Michelet's History of the French Revolution (1).

Thiers. History of the Consulate and Empire of France under Napoleon (1).

The production of the best of French historians, whose faithfulness and industry as a reliable chronicler of the events of this the "brightest of the days of France," render the present work valuable as well as interesting to the student.

Bourienne. Life of Napoleon (2).

Hazlitt. Life of Napoleon (1).

A work of much vigor and power, though prejudiced. It is the most elaborate work of this author.

Sir Walter Scott's Life of Napoleon (2).

This is another history of that awful event, the French Revolution, written by a master hand. I have entire confidence in its fidelity, and undissembled admiration of the wisdom of his reflections, the neatness and purity of his style, and the eloquence of his descriptive powers. It may be, that when writers of brilliant genius undertake to write sober history, there is some danger that they may unconsciously impart to their narrations some of the creations of a rich and fervid imagination. Such historians were Herodotus, Livy, Vertot, Voltaire, Burke, Sismondi, Scott, and Irving.—*Kent.*

Las Casas. Life of Napoleon at St. Helena (1).

Memoirs Dictated at St. Helena.

Cockburn, Sir Geo. Diary of the Voyage of Bonaparte (2).

Maitland. Narrative of the Voyage in the Bellerophon (2).

These works, read in connection, will give the reader all of the different versions of the captivity of Napoleon, and enable him to form a just estimate of that part of the life of "the Emperor."—*Ch. King.*

Montholon's Captivity of Napoleon at St. Helena (2).

Segur's Napoleon's Expedition to Russia (1).

Written by one who, from the nature of his literary habits and tastes, and the vivacity of his character, would be deemed most able to describe all that he had observed.—*Am. Quar. Rev.*

Abbott's Life of Josephine (1).

Memoirs of Josephine, with Anecdotes.

Every thing connected with the life of this noble woman cannot fail to command attention.

Alison's History of Europe (1). (*See page* 14.)

Burke's Letters on the French Revolution (1).

Headley, J. T. Napoleon and his Marshals (2).

A dashing, spirited book, whose brilliant sketches and vivid coloring are well calculated to attract and please; though its views of character, and hasty and unconsidered opinions, render it unreliable as a part of History.

Lamartine. The Restoration in France (2).

The latest historical production of this brilliant historian, written in his usual flowing and florid style.

Cass, Lewis. France, its King, Court and Government (1).

An agreeably written Memoir of the Court of Louis Philippe, and of his family circle, into which our then Minister in France, Gen. Cass, seems to have been admitted with great intimacy.—*Ch. King.*

Blanc, Louis. France under Louis Philippe, from 1830 *to* 1840 (3).

A work by a contemporary, who might be styled a permanent conspirator against the government and political system which he describes. Its narrative is spirited, but its deductions are to be received with caution.—*Ch. King.*

Child, Mrs. L. M. Memoirs of Madame de Stael and Madame Roland (2).

Lamballe, Princess de. Secret Memoirs of French Revolution (2).

La Rochejacquelin, Marchioness de, Memoirs of (2).

Interesting memoirs, that will well repay perusal.

V. ENGLAND.

General.

Henry's History of Great Britain (2).

Carries the narration down to the death of Henry VIII. It is written on a new plan, and separates the civil and military history of each volume from the ecclesiastical history, and from that of the laws, the learning, the arts, commerce, and manners of the same period. The history is compiled with great erudition and fidelity, and the plan has been highly extolled, but his style is not attractive, nor has the capricious taste of the public rescued the work from neglect.—*Kent.*

Hume's History of England (2),

With Smollett's Continuation. [This has been further continued by Bisset, by Miller, and by Hughes.]

The accuracy of Hume, in respect to the two first princes of the house of Stuart, has been severely attacked by G. Stuart, Whitaker, Brodie, and others; but his charming style, his profound sagacity, and his philosophical reflections, clothe his great work with irresistible attractions.—*Kent.*

Goldsmith's History of England.

Is a beautiful sketch.

Turner's History of England (2),
Down to the Lives of the Tudors.

Is replete with Anglo-Saxon and other ancient learning; and it is written with dignity, purity, and eloquence. Turner surpasses Hume in the depth and fulness of his researches, and in the spirit and tenor of his moral reflections.—*Kent.*

Sir James Mackintosh's History of England (1),
From the Roman Conquest to the Reign of Elizabeth.

It is an excellent summary of the most memorable events in English history, and contains a sound and philosophical view of the nature and progress of her social and political institutions, written in a chaste and elegant style.—*Kent.*

Lingard, Dr. History of England (3).

Is the work of a diligent and learned (Roman Catholic) writer, whose style is concise and perspicuous, and who discusses subjects with acuteness and force, and candor. He is charged, however, by Protestant writers with being disturbed in the exercise of his accustomed impartiality when on religious subjects.—*Kent.*

Craik and McFarlane (continued by Harriet Martineau).
Pictorial History of England (1).

Macaulay's History of England,
From the Accession of James 2d.

"Macaulay," says the Edinburgh Review," is the first historian who has succeeded in giving to the realities of history (which is generally supposed to demand and require a certain grave austerity of style) the lightness, variety, and attraction of a work designed only to amuse. To read other historians is a study, an effort of the intellect, but with our author, even on the most beaten ground, his power of picturesque description brings out lights and shadows—views alike of distances, and of roadside flowers—never seen, or remarked, or recollected before."

We cannot, however, but add, that many of the conclusions of this author are discolored by prejudice and partiality; and the reader should not allow himself to be too much captivated by the great felicity of his style, of which there is much danger.

Keightley's History of England (1).

Special Portions of English History.

The histories of detached portions of English history are very numerous. Of them I will mention—

Thierry. History of the Conquest of England by the Normans (2).

A stirring and eloquent history, by a Frenchman, of one of the few conquests which has left its impress upon all future time, and upon a teeming race of men.

Burnet. History of his own Times (2).

A courtier, a bishop, and a statesman—these Memoirs exhibit traces of all these characters.—*Ch. King.*

Clarendon's History of the Rebellion and Civil Wars under Charles 1st (2).

This history has had great renown, but has been severely criticised and depreciated in the present age. The style is bad, with long and most tiresome periods; but the candid reader will be forcibly struck with the moderation of the author, and his strong and impressive sketches of character. The state papers interspersed in the volumes, are drawn with an ability and perspicuity that would do honor to any age; and the leading actors in those turbulent and revolutionary scenes were men of the greatest genius and most exalted endowments.—*Kent.*

Godwin's History of the Commonwealth of England (2).

Is a political counterpart of that of Lord Clarendon; for the writer was of the radical school of politics, and of the atheistical school of philosophy. —*Kent.*

Guizot's English Revolution of 1688 (1).
Translated by Mrs. Austin.

The work of an accomplished scholar, a courteous inquirer, and a practised statesman.

Mackintosh's History of the Revolution in England of 1688 (1).

Neal. History of the Puritans (2).

A work of considerable authority, and reflects much credit upon the talents of the author.—*Blake's Biog. Dict.*

Forster, John. Life of Cromwell (1).

As abridged in the Westminster Review, for October, 1839, is masterly —*Kent.*

Southey's Life of Cromwell (1).

Lyttleton's History of the Reign of Henry 2d.

It is heavy, prolix, but trustworthy; and contains searching investigations into the laws, policy, characters, and events of that reign.—*Kent.*

Halsted, Caroline. History of Richard 3d (2).

Curious, but full of interest, as giving a different view of the life of a man to whom history seems to have resolved to deny justice.

Bacon's History of Henry 7th (3).

It is short, and nothing striking, except that it bears the name of Bacon. —*Kent.*

Aikin, Miss. Memoirs of the Court of Elizabeth (2),

And that of James, and that of Charles 1st, are delightfully entertaining, and equally distinguished for sagacity, taste, accuracy, candor, and elegant and graphic delineation of character.—*Kent.*

Thomson, Mrs. Memoirs of Sarah, Duchess of Marlborough (2), *and of the Court of Queen Anne.*

Always a period of interest. Macaulay's late work, with its truculent judgments, and pictured narration, adds fresh interest to these Memoirs.

Croly's Life and Times of George the Fourth (3).

This is well written, but the subject of the historian was a profligate man.—*Kent.*

Strickland, Agnes. The Queens of England (2).

Full of valuable information, though not always true to history.

Southey's Early Naval History of England (2).

Learned, entertaining, and authentic.—*Kent.*

James. Naval History of England (3).

De Foe. The History of the Great Plague in London, in 1665.

Written with all the author's renowned skill and graphic power; it is not, however, to be mistaken for authentic history.

Campbell's Lives of the Lord Chancellors (2).

Mahon, Lord. History of England, from the Peace of Utrecht (2).

Hallam's Constitutional History of England (1).

VI. SCOTLAND.

Scott, Sir W. History of Scotland (1).

Tytler. History of Scotland (2).

Robertson's History of Scotland (2), *during the Reign of Mary, and*

Stuart, Gilbert. History of Scotland (2), *during the same period.*

These are antagonist histories, and each of them is written with very great elegance and dignity.—*Kent.*

Buchanan, Geo. History of Scotland (3).

As a historian, he is considered to have united the beauties of Livy and Sallust as to style; but he discovered a great lack of judgment and investigative spirit, taking up all the tales of the chronicles as he found them, and affording to their legendary absurdities the currency of his own eloquent embellishments. He wrote in the early part of the 16th century.—*Bp. Potter.*

Strickland, Agnes. The Queens of Scotland (2).
Now in course of publication.

Mignet. History of Mary, Queen of Scots (2).

A most interesting history of this beautiful but unfortunate Queen. It possesses much value for its full and authentic historical information.

Abbott's Sketch of her Life, and Bell's Life of the Queen, are also valuable and interesting works.

Brown's History of the Highland Clans.

Jesse's Memoirs of the Pretenders and their Adherents (2).

Chambers, R. History of the Rebellions in Scotland (1).

VII. IRELAND.

Leland's History of Ireland (2).

Dr. Leland commences his history with the Invasion of Ireland by Henry II., and he carries it down to the Revolution in 1688. It is written with judgment, care, and just discrimination. The historian was Prebendary of St. Patrick's, Dublin.—*Kent.*

Moore, Thomas. History of Ireland (1).

Well recommended, and worthy of confidence.

Taylor's History of Ireland (1).

Musgrave's Memoirs of the Rebellions in Ireland.

VIII. SPAIN AND PORTUGAL.

Calcott, Mrs. History of Spain (2).

Every thing is done that can be done by good sense and good principles of civil and religious liberty, and by commendable diligence in the collection and display of the materials which her subject supplied: and the student will see the main points presented to his view, and reasonable observations made, and on the whole feel his mind left in a state of sufficient repose and satisfaction with respect to this portion of his course of historical reading.—*Smyth.*

Vertot, The Abbé. Revolutions of Spain and Portugal (3).

Are very interesting, and have the charms of romance with the gravity and fidelity of history. They are written with great elegance. The work on Portugal gives the history of the deliverance of Portugal from the yoke of Spain, and the restoration of the house of Braganza, and it does great credit to the energy and patriotism of the Portuguese character.—*Kent.*

Robertson's History of the Reign of the Emperor Charles V. (1).

Watson's History of the Reign of Philip II. and Philip III. (1).

Prescott's History of Ferdinand and Isabella (1).

Irving's Life and Voyages of Columbus (1).

These works illustrate a period the most splendid in Spanish history, and are sterling productions of the highest order.

Dunham's History of Spain and Portugal (2).

Napier's History of the Peninsular War (1), *and*

Southey's History of the Peninsular War (2).

Are histories of eminent reputation. Napier's is by far the most authentic and interesting, being written by an able military man.

Florian. History of the Moors (2).

Facility, grace, harmony, and a sensibility rare in the French character, are the most striking characteristics of his works. His descriptions of manners are striking and faithful.—*Enc. Am.*

Irving. Conquest of Grenada (1).

The History of the Moors in Spain, could not have been penned by any one whose peculiar talents were better suited to his subject. It gives the history of a people whose memory has almost passed away, but the remains of whose magnificence still attract the attention of the world, and whose influence is yet visible upon the intellectual culture of Europe.—*N. Amer. Rev.*

Laclede. History of Portugal.

Mahon, Lord. War of the Succession in Spain (2).

—— ——— *Spain under Charles II.* (2).

IX. SWITZERLAND.

Von Muller. History of Switzerland (2).

Vieusseux. History of Switzerland (2).

The History of Switzerland (1). (Lardner's Cyclopædia.)

Zchokke's Popular History of Switzerland (1).

X. TURKEY AND GREECE.

Knolles. General History of the Turks (2).

Urquhart. Turkey and its Resources (1).

Macfarlane. Turkey and its Destiny (1).

Keightley's Greek War of Independence (1).

Gordon. History of the Greek Revolution (2).

Ranke's History of the Ottoman and Spanish Empires in the 16th and 17th Centuries (2).

Taylor, W. C. History of Mohammedanism (1).

XI. RUSSIA AND POLAND.

Tooke's History of Russia (2).

This work proceeds from the foundation of the monarchy to the accession of Catharine II.

He has also published the History of the Reign of Catharine II. He is a respectable historian.—*Kent.*

Bell's History of Russia (1).

Voltaire. History of Russia under Peter the Great (2), *and*

Castrera. History of Catharine II. (2).

The former is lively—the latter a grave and impressive story.—*Kent.*

Barrow's Life of Peter the Great (1).

Coxe's Russian Discoveries (2).

Contains the history of the conquest of Siberia by Russia, in the 16th century, and which brought that empire in collision with China.—*Kent.*

Kohl J. G. Russia, St. Petersburgh, &c. (2).

Fletcher. History of Poland (1).

Corner. History of Poland.

Palmer's Life of Sobieski.

Dunham. History of Poland (1).

XII. HOLLAND, DENMARK, SWEDEN, AND NORWAY.

Davies. History of Holland (1).

Grattan. History of the Netherlands (1).

Schiller. Revolt of the Netherlands (1).

Chricton and Wheaton. History of Denmark, Sweden, and Norway (1).

The joint productions of two of the ripest scholars in Punic literature.

Vertot's Revolution in Sweden (2).

Gives the life of Gustavus Vasa, the deliverer of his country, and who in the mountains of Dalecarlia roused his countrymen to arms. The Abbé de Mably considered that this history of Sweden would bear a comparison with the finest morsels of antiquity.—*Kent.*

Harté. Life of Gustavus Adolphus (2).

Voltaire. History of Charles XII. (2).

Andrews. History of the Danish Revolution (1).

Dunham. History of Denmark (1).

Murray's Hand-Book for Northern Europe (2).

XIII. ASIATIC AND AFRICAN POWERS.

Chricton. History of Arabia (1).

Frazer. History of Persia (1).

Mavor. History of the Arabs (2).

——— *History of the Ottoman Empire in Asia.*

Kent.

Ockley. History of the Saracens (1).

A full, faithful, and interesting history of this remarkable race.

Irving, Washington. Mahomet and his Successors (2).

In which the author strives to rescue his hero from the imputation of being a mere impostor, and to rank him among useful and fortunate reformers.

Russell's History of Palestine (1).

This volume contains a topographical description of the Holy Land as it exists at present, and a full history of the wonderful people by whom it was anciently possessed.

Robertson's Disquisition concerning Ancient India (1).

"Excellent."—*Kent.*

Dow's History of Hindostan (2).

Mavor. History of Hindostan (3).

Murray's Historical Account of British India (1).

Gleig's History of the British Empire in India (2).

Taylor, W. C. Popular History of British India (1).

Raffles's History of Java (1).

This is a great work of the utmost accuracy and authenticity; and gives a better account of the geography, resources, population, character, commerce, arts, and history of the half-civilized inhabitants of a great and flourishing native empire, than any other work extant.—*Kent.*

Marsden's History of the Immense Island of Sumatra (2),

With its fierce and barbarous native powers, is another work of high character and deep interest.—*Kent.*

Thornton. History of China (2).

Du Halde. History of China (2).

This is the work of a learned and pious Jesuit. It is ample in description, and is written with great simplicity and judgment.—*Kent.*

Bell of Antermony—his Travels (2).

He went with the Russian embassy under Ismayloff from Petersburg to Pekin, in 1720, to the court of Kamhi, the emperor of China; is about as curious, honest, intelligent, and interesting a narration, as any extant.—*Kent.*

Medhurst. China and its State and Prospects (1).

The author was a member of the London Missionary Society, and his work is authentic and very valuable.

Gutzlaff's Sketch of Chinese History and Trade (1).

Is also an authentic and interesting picture of China, and reflects credit on the zeal, diligence, knowledge, and great merits of the author. I may here add, that there is an article in the American Quarterly Review, No. 33, on Chinese history (and of which this work is the text), which may be considered as a learned and masterly production.—*Kent.*

Williams, S. Wells. Middle Kingdom; or, a Survey of the Chinese Empire (1).

A recent work, full of curious and valuable information, and written in a graceful and pleasing style. Its author, an American, had many opportunities of observation and study.

Downing. The Stranger in China (2).

Gives a novel and interesting account of the domestic life and manners of the Chinese.

Davis's History of China (1).

Is also trustworthy and comprehensive.

Ellis's History of Madagascar (1).

Is a full and very valuable account of that great island, abounding in impervious forests, and inhabited by millions of half civilized black and olive races of men, susceptible of higher improvement.—*Kent.*

Greenhow's History of Tripoli.

Shaler's Sketches of Algiers.

Jackson's Account of the Empire of Morocco.

Are all of them authentic, creditable, and instructive publications.—*Kent.*

Russell. History of the Barbary States (1).

Macfarlane. Account of Japan (1).

XIV. AMERICAN HISTORY.

United States, generally.

Burke's European Settlements in America (2).

Chalmers. Political Annals of the United Colonies, From their first Settlement in 1763 (2).

Much esteemed.—*Kent.*

Bancroft's History of the United States (1).

There is very much to admire in the research and style of this work. It is well and powerfully written, and deserves to take rank as the most reliable work on the subject.

Grahame's History of North America (2).

This is a European production, and it is written with great gravity and dignity, moderation and justice.—*Kent.*

Pitkin's History of the United States,
From 1763 to 1797 (2).

This is an accurate and trustworthy production, and Mr. Pitkin has filled high public trusts and sustained a pure and excellent character.—*Kent.*

Marshall's Life of Washington (1).
Volume I., on Colonial History.—*Kent.*

Hildreth, Richard. History of the United States (1).

A recent work, faithfully written, and which adds very much to the historical renown of our country.

Catlin's North American Indians (3).

Hawks, Rev. Francis, LL. D. Contributions to the Ecclesiastical History of the United States (2).

Very explanatory of our colonial condition, and of the many difficulties in the way of our independence.—*Ch. King.*

Holmes, Abiel. Annals of America (2).

Blunt, Jos. Historical Sketch of the Formation of the American Confederacy (3).

A careful, patient, and true exposition of the motives and aims of the great men, who in the confederacy laid the foundation of our Union.—*Ch. King.*

Cabot, Sebastian. Memoir (2).
Prepared and edited by the late Richard Biddle, of Pittsburg.

The work of a distinguished American scholar and statesman. It is well deserving of study.

Irving's Life of Columbus (1).

Hamilton's Works.

Madison's Papers.

Adams, John. Life and Writings.

2*

Adams, Mrs. Letters.

Adams, Miss. Letters.

Adams, John Quincy. The Jubilee of the Constitution.

All of these are most important sources of information for a student of American history. The character and motives of many of the principal men who formed this republic are thus displayed to us unreservedly, and the works of the Adamses especially exhibit such an uncompromising love of liberty, such indomitable firmness amid great danger, and so much patriotism, that they cannot be studied without warming the heart, and confirming the love of country of young Americans.—*Ch. King.*

Parkman, Francis, Jr. History of the Conspiracy of Pontiac (2).

A fine narrative of stirring periods and events in our aboriginal history. —*Ch. King.*

Cooper's History of the Navy of the United States (2).

A plain, frank, unpretending narration.—*Kent.*

Sullivan, Wm. Familiar Letters on Public Characters and Events, from 1783 to 1815 (2).

Gibbs, George. Administrations of Washington and Adams (2).

A contribution from the papers of Oliver Wolcott, the successor of Alexander Hamilton as Secretary of the Treasury of the United States, arranged and prepared with boldness and talent by his grandson, of inestimable value for its authentic materials.—*Ch. King.*

Findlay. Insurrection in the Four Western Counties of Pennsylvania.

Cobbett, Wm. Peter Porcupine's Works.

Vindictive, bold, and unscrupulous. Cobbett in these volumes has left a picture of the politics and of some of the leading politicians of America, from 1783 to 1801, which must be studied (with abundant caution against the spirit in which they are written) by all, who would understand the party questions which then agitated America, and the violence with which they were discussed.—*Ch. King.*

Debates in the House of Representatives,

On the British Treaty in 1795.

These debates, conducted in part by the framers of the Constitution, or more truly the framer, John Jay, so much vilified at the time, so prolific of blessings afterwards, established its true construction on that head of the Constitution.—*Ch. King.*

HISTORIES OF THE SEVERAL STATES.

Belknap's History of New Hampshire.

The first volume appeared in Philadelphia in 1784. This work was reprinted in England, and mentioned in the periodical literature of the day in very respectful terms. Being one of our earliest domestic histories, it was received in this country with peculiar respect.—*Kent.*

Hutchinson's History of Massachusetts.

This was a colonial publication, and one very respectable.—*Kent.*

Winthrop's Journal.

Edited by SAVAGE.

This work relates to the first settlement of Massachusetts and the other New England colonies. The notes of the learned editor add greatly to its interest and value.—*Kent.*

Morton's New England Memorial.

Edited by Judge DAVIS.

This history is a curiosity in several respects. It was the earliest history of New England, and confined principally to the Plymouth colony. It was compiled upon the recommendation of the commissioners of the four united colonies of New England, in 1656; and the object was "to collect the special and remarkable passages of God's providence towards them."—*Kent.*

Bayley's Historical Memoir of the Colony of New Plymouth.

A very respectable work.—*Kent.*

Trumbull's History of Connecticut.

This history commences with the first settlement of the colony, and it is brought down to 1764. It is a work of substantial merit and uncommon interest. As the first settlers were intelligent, learned, pious, and discreet pilgrims, they established a republic of the most simple and perfect kind, and furnished it with a code of popular instruction and of civil and religious discipline, and of social institutions, and of order and decorum unparalleled in the history of mankind. The colonial republic of Connecticut, as represented in this work, is a phenomenon in the history of civil society.—*Kent.*

Mather, Cotton. Magnalia Christi Amer.; or, Ecclesiastical History of New England.

Is to the student of the early annals of New England, indispensable. It is alike genial in style and sentiment.—*Ch. King.*

Williams's History of Vermont.

Kent.

Smith's History of New-York.

The first volume was compiled in 1756, and the second volume, which brings the history down to 1762, was a posthumous publication. The author died at Quebec in 1793, and was then chief justice of Canada. The work is sensibly written, and with perfect authenticity; but it is as dry as ordinary annals.

See also Dunlap's History of New-York, 2 vols. 8vo., 1840, and Col. Stone's History of Brant, the celebrated Mohawk Chief. Interesting.—*Kent.*

McCaulay. Natural, Statistical, and Civil History of New-York.

A heavy work, yet may be consulted for facts.—*Ch. King.*

Hammond, Jabez. Political History of New-York.

Pains-taking, but not always accurate.—*Ch. King.*

O'Callaghan, E. B. History of New Netherlands (1).

——— *Documentary History of the State of New-York.*

Both of these works are well worthy of study; they contain much curious and valuable information, are well written, and with ability. The last is still in progress.

Gordon's History of New Jersey.

Kent.

Proud's History of Pennsylvania, from 1681 *to* 1742.

This work is of great research, and abounds with valuable matter; but "it is the most confused and tedious composition that ever tormented human patience."—*Kent.*

Stith's History of Virginia.

Kent.

Howison's History of Virginia (1).

Howe's History of Virginia.

Williamson's History of North Carolina.

Kent.

Pickett. History of Alabama.

Marbois. History of Louisiana.

A French colony described by a clever Frenchman.—*Ch. King.*

Gayarre. History of Louisiana (1).

Called a romance, but impressing facts.—*Ch. King.*

Irving, Theodore. The Conquest of Florida.

Lanman's History of Michigan.

Excellent.—*Kent.*

Monetté. History of the Mississippi Valley.

Flint's History and Geography of the Mississippi Valley.

Kent.

Tanner. View of the Valley of the Mississippi.

Excellent.—*Kent.*

Forbes's History of California. 1838.

A work of superior excellence and most useful instruction. North California is the most attractive country on the west side of the American continent, between the arctic and antarctic regions.—*Kent.*

The publications of the Historical Societies of the different States may also be consulted as affording much information relative to the history of the States, not to be found elsewhere: those of Massachusetts, New-York, New Hampshire, and New Jersey, are particularly valuable.

THE AMERICAN REVOLUTION.

Hildreth. History of the United States (2).

Botta's History of the War of Independence (2).

Mr. Jay was reading this history when I visited him in 1820; and he told me that its general accuracy was undoubted.—*Kent.*

Lossing, Bernard J. Pictorial Field-Book of the Revolution (1).

Now in course of publication.

Washington's Writings, by Sparks (1).

Bancroft's United States (1).

The 4th and 5th volumes commence the History of the Revolution.

Heath, Maj. Gen. Wm. Memoirs of Events during the American War.

Thatcher, Dr. S. Military Journal during the American Revolution.

Moultré, Wm. Memoirs of the American Revolution.

Ramsay's History of the Revolution in South Carolina.

General Greene (and there could not be a better witness) vouched for the accuracy of this history.—*Kent.*

Lee's Memoirs of the War in the Southern Department of the United States.

They are very interesting, and as fascinating as a romance, though they undoubtedly contain true history.—*Kent.*

Drayton, John. Memoirs of the American Revolution relating to South Carolina.

Tarleton, Lieut. Col. B. History of the Campaigns of 1780–81 *in the Southern Provinces of North America.*

Simcoe's Journal. History of the Queen's Rangers.

Ch. King.

Frothingam. Siege of Boston, and Battles of Lexington and Concord.—Ch. King.

Campbell, Wm. W. Annals of Tryon County; or, Border Warfare of New-York.

Washington and his Generals.

By various hands.

Trumbull, Col. John. Autobiographical Reminiscences, and Letters from 1756 *to* 1841.

Sanderson's Signers of the Declaration of Independence.

Ch. King.

Curwen's Journal and Letters, from 1775—1784.

Van Schaick, Henry C. Life of Peter Van Schaick.

The two last, interesting as showing the views of honest and able men, American-born, against the separation of the colonies from the mother country. The name of Tory is even yet a brand. These volumes show how Tories acted upon their honest convictions received and asked.—*Ch. King.*

Sparks, Jared. Diplomatic Correspondence of the American Revolution.

For occasional consultation and refreshment, when it is desired to verify any facts, or renew the self-sacrificing patriotism which made that revolution successful.—*Ch. King.*

Jones's Defence of North Carolina.

A clever controversial tract, vindicating the authenticity of the Mecklenburgh Declaration of Independence in 1776, before that made 4th July in Philadelphia.—*Ch. King.*

Publications of the New-York Historical Society.

War of 1812.

Ingersoll, Charles J. History of the War of 1812 (2).

A partisan book, and therefore to be read with hesitation; but of undoubted ability and information.

Breckenbridge. History of the War of 1812 (1).

Armstrong. War of 1812 (1).

America—its Glory as exemplified in the War of 1812.

Wilkinson, Gen. Memoirs.

Hull's Campaign and Court Martial, and Hull's Defence.

Pickering, T. Political Essays in 1812.

Christie, R. Military and Naval Operations in Canada during the War of 1812.

Clairborne. Notes on the War in the South;
With Sketches of Jackson.

Dwight, Theodore. History of the Hartford Convention.

Van Rensselaer, Gen. Solomon. Narrative of the Affair at Queenstown.

Perkins. An Historical Sketch of the United States since 1812.

All to be consulted, or read, with the official documents of the times in order to obtain a just appreciation of the war of 1812.—*Ch. King.*

Burgess. Battles of Lake Erie.

Elliott, Commodore—Biography of.

Mackenzie, Alex. Slidell. Life of Commodore Perry.

The brilliant victory of Lake Erie was for years after its occurrence a source of crimination and recrimination as to relative merits of the first and second in command; the three publications, above named, leave little doubt of the soundness of the popular opinion, which makes Perry the hero of the victory.—*Ch. King.*

The Mexican War.

Mansfield's Mexican War (2).
Ch. King.

Ripley, Maj. R. S. The War in Mexico (1).
The most comprehensive History of the War that has yet appeared.

Henry, W. S. *Campaign Sketches of the War in Mexico.*
Ch. King.

Carleton, J. H. *The Battle of Buena Vista.*

Thorpe. *Our Army on the Rio Grande.*

——— *Our Army at Monterey.*

These several works give a full and authentic account of the recent war with Mexico, and can be referred to as the most reliable authority that have yet appeared on this subject.

Ramsey. *The Other Side of the American War* (2).
Translated from the Spanish.

Jay, William. *Causes and Consequences of the Mexican War* (1).

This last work is in regard to the origin of the War, and its motives;—strong and emphatic, but hardly impartial.—*Ch. King.*

XV. OTHER PARTS OF AMERICA.

Haliburton's Account of Nova Scotia.
Kent.

Bouchette's Description of Canada.
Kent.

Hawkins's Historical Recollections of Canada and Quebec.
Excellent.—*Kent.*

Humboldt on New Spain.
Translated by BLACK.—*Kent.*

Robertson's History of America (1).

This history is the most attractive of all Dr. Robertson's productions. Criticism has detected imperfections and errors, but it has not shaken the solidity of the fabric.—*Kent.*

Irving's History of the Life and Voyages of Columbus (1).

This work is founded partly on access to new and original documents in Spain; and it is written with the attractions of style and taste, and glowing description, which belong to the inspiration of the theme, and to the genius of the distinguished author.—*Kent.*

Southey's History of Brazil (1).

Kent.

History of the Buccaneers.

This is a work for heroic enterprise and remorseless daring, unparalleled in the tales of romance.—*Kent.*

Edwards's History of the British Colonies in the West Indies.

A learned and elegant work.—*Kent.*

Franklin's Present State of Hayti, 1828.

Kent.

Brown's History and Present Condition of St. Domingo, 1837.—*Kent.*

History of Chili, by Molini.

Translated by Alsop, 1808.

It is a work of respectable character.—*Kent.*

Cortes, Letters and Dispatches of.

Translated by Geo. Folsom.

Very curious and interesting, being the original letters, transmitted by the daring conqueror to his government. They have been finely translated by Mr. Folsom.

Warburton, Eliot. The Conquest of Canada (2).

A recent work, by an accomplished writer, and well worthy of attention.

Prescott's Conquest of Peru (1).

Fully equal in interest to the other historical works of Mr. Prescott. He is remarkable for his effective arrangement of facts, and the felicitous manner in which he explores every source of information relating to his subjects.

Prescott. Conquest of Mexico.

The Conquest of Mexico, by Cortes, forms one of those romantic episodes in history, which give color to the saying, that "Truth is stranger than fiction." The materials upon which this work was founded, were drawn from the original documents in the possession of the government of Spain. It is written in a clear and perspicuous style, and as a historical production, deserves to take the very highest rank. It is regarded as the most popular production of its author.

Cuba and the Cubans.

III.

BIOGRAPHY.

I. BIOGRAPHICAL DICTIONARIES.

Biographie Universelle.

The great French work, with continuation, in all about 80 vols.

Rose's Biographical Dictionary, 12 vols. (1).

Chalmers's Biographical Dictionary.

Gorton's Biographical Dictionary, 4 vols.

The best portable work for ordinary reference, is Parke Godwin's "Handbook of Biography,"—one of Putnam's "Home Cyclopædias."

II. AMERICAN BIOGRAPHY.

Sparks's Life and Writings of Washington (1).

Nothing can equal, at least to an American reader, the interest and excellence of this work: its perfect accuracy and impartiality, and the simplicity, greatness and grandeur of Washington's character.—*Kent.*

Marshall's Life of Washington (1).

This work is very authentic and accurate, except the first volume on Colonial History. It is written with great simplicity and perspicuity, but it has lost much of its interest and attraction since the appearance of Sparks's immortal work.—*Kent.*

Sparks's Works of Franklin, with his Life (1).

Here is the historical portrait, admirably designed, of another American statesman, of pre-eminent good sense and simplicity of character, and whose fair fame has shed lustre on his country.—*Kent.*

Guizot. Character of Washington (1).
From the French.

Jay, P. A. The Life of John Jay.
By his Son.—*Kent.*

Sparks's Life of Gouverneur Morris.
Kent.

Sedgwick. The Life of William Livingston.
Kent.

The Life of Alexander Hamilton.
By his Son.

These four last biographical works contain the lives of illustrious statesmen, who have adorned the annals of this country, and rendered their names immortal by their services, their patriotism, and their distinguished talents, in the great crisis of the American revolution.—*Kent.*

Delaplaine's Distinguished Americans.

Precious memorials of the men and times of the Revolution,—our heroic age,—with which we cannot be too familiar, for its spirit was lofty.—*Ch. King.*

Hosack's Memoir of De Witt Clinton.
Kent.

Wheaton's Life of William Pinckney.
Kent.

Wirt's Life of Patrick Henry (1).
Kent.

Tudor's Life of Otis.

Kent.

Sparks's Life of Ledyard, the Traveller.

Kent.

Stone's Life of Brant.

Kent.

Belknap's American Biography.

Kent.

Sparks's American Biography (2).

25 vols. Two series.—*Kent.*

Johnson, Wm. Life and Correspondence of General Nathaniel Greene.

Lee, Gen. Charles. Memoirs, Essays, and Letters.

Lee was an Englishman whose previous military experience gave him high rank in the revolutionary army. Disgraced for misconduct at the battle of Monmouth in 1778, he left the service, and amused his leisure as a planter in Virginia, and by splenetic writings against General Washington and the American army. To be read as a part of history.—*Ch. King.*

Tucker's Life of Jefferson.

Ch. King.

Dwight, Theodore. Character of Jefferson.

Ch. King.

Lee, H. Observations on the Life of Jefferson.

Mr. Jefferson is and ever will remain one of the great figures among the founders of this nation. Hence no one of the Fathers of the country has been more vehemently praised and abused.—*Kent.*

Davis, M. L. Life of Aaron Burr.

This is generally esteemed the best biography of this great statesman extant. See also a review of the same in the New-York Review.—*Kent.*

Duer, W. A. Life of Lord Stirling.

An interesting biographical sketch of an ardent patriot of the Revolution, by a lineal descendant.—*Kent.*

Austin, Jas. T. Life of Elbridge Gerry.

Kirkland, J. T. Life of Fisher Ames.

Colden, Cadwalader D. Life of Robert Fulton.

Kennedy, J. P. Life of William Wirt (1).

Mackenzie, Alex. Slidell. Life of Paul Jones.

Sherburne, J. H. Life of Paul Jones.

Eaton, J. H. Life of Andrew Jackson.

Dawson, Moses. Life and Services of W. H. Harrison.

Colton, Calvin. Life and Speeches of Henry Clay.

Quincy, Josiah. Memoirs of Josiah Quincy.

All of these works should be read as forming a part of the history of our country. Admiration for the lives of those who have rendered the "state good service" ought to be encouraged—it is a noble incentive to young and ardent minds.

Grant, Mrs. Memoirs of an American Lady (1).

A faithful narrative of the manner and modes of life of the ante-revolutionary residents of Albany chiefly.—*Ch. King.*

Dunlap, Wm. G. Life of Charles Brockden Brown.

Ware, John. Memoir of Henry Ware, Jr.

Lee, Mrs. E. B. Lives of the Buckminsters.

Channing, W. H. Life of William Ellery Channing.

The life of a pure-minded man is ever interesting, and we know of no work that can be read with greater profit than the life of this Christian philanthropist and philosopher.

Garland's Life of John Randolph (1).

Many more biographical sketches, principally of characters in private professions and literary life, well worthy of perusal, might be suggested, but I have deemed the foregoing selection sufficiently extensive to give the reader a well-informed view of the lives of some of the more distinguished of Americans.—*Ed.*

III. EUROPEAN.

Boswell's Life of Johnson (1).

Edited by JOHN WILSON CROKER.

One of the most attractive and perhaps complete biographical memoirs ever published.

Prior's Life of Burke (2).

A comprehensive view of the life of England's most worthy statesman.

———— *Life of Goldsmith* (1).

Irving, W. Oliver Goldsmith; a Biography (1).

Truly fascinating memoirs of one of the most interesting of men, whose kindness of heart should ever commend him to the charity of his readers.

Southey's Life of Nelson (1).

The most delightful and perhaps the most durable of all Southey's productions.—*Kent.*

———— *Life of Cowper* (1).

Kent.

Thomson, Mrs. A. T. Life of Sir Walter Raleigh.

The life of a man who has connected his name indelibly with our own land, and whose life, accomplishments, virtues, and misfortunes invest his memory with all the charm of romance.

Walton, Isaak. Lives of Donne, Wotton, Hooker, &c. (1).

Written with the truest benevolence, and without pretension, and dear to all lovers of simplicity of style, and of unaffected learning.

Cumberland's Memoirs.

Written by himself.—*Kent.*

Otter's Life of Edward D. Clarke, the Traveller.

A work of the most intense interest.—*Ch. King.*

Dixon, Hepworth. Life of William Penn.

To be read with especial interest by Americans since the attacks of Macaulay upon the character of the venerated founder of Pennsylvania; for the character of Penn in this work is most successfully vindicated, and stands out in broader light even than heretofore, as a public man of fine cultivation, moral address, high aims, and large and liberal views.—*Ch. King.*

Le Bas. Life of Wicklif (1).

——— *Life of Cranmer* (1).

Biographies of men of strong will and earnest purpose, whose labors, talents, and devotedness, changed the face of the world.—*Ch. King.*

——— *Life of Jewell.*

——— *Life of Laud.*

Forbes, Sir Wm. Life of James Beattie.
Ch. King.

Teignmouth's Life of Sir William Jones.
Ch. King.

Sir Humphrey Davy's Life.
By his Brother.—*Kent.*

Lockhart. Life of Burns (2).

The most complete memoir of this distinguished author.

Chambers. Life and Works of Burns.

Lockhart. ·Life of Sir Walter Scott.

The most impressive and instructive life, and one that awakens the tenderest sympathies.—*Kent.*

Moore, Thos. Life of Sheridan.

An interesting memoir of this most gifted orator and dramatist.

Gleig, G. A. Memoirs of Warren Hastings.
Ch. King.

——— *Life of Lord Clive.*

Ch. King.

Life of Mrs. Siddons (2).
By CAMPBELL.—*Kent.*

Duke of Wellington, The Despatches of.
Compiled by GURWOOD.

The most authentic and valuable of biographical productions. It is analogous to Sparks's Life and Writings of Washington.—*Kent.*

Gibbon, The Autobiographical Life of (2).

The first volume of his miscellaneous works, is most delightful and most instructive, as to the value of time, and the growing stimulus of genius. —*Kent.*

Brougham's Sketches of Eminent Statesmen under George III.—*Kent.*

Cunningham's Lives of the most Eminent Painters.
Kent.

Heber, Bishop. Life.
By his Widow.—*Kent.*

Brewster. Life of Sir Isaac Newton.
Kent.

Stewart's Life of Dr. Robertson.
Kent.

Wilberforce's Life (1).
By his Son.—*Kent.*

Scott's Biographical Memoirs of Eminent Novelists.
Kent.

Scott's Life of Swift (1).
Kent.

Scott's Life of Dryden (1).
Kent.

Talfourd, Th. N. Life and Letters of Charles Lamb (1).

——— *Final Memorials of Charles Lamb.*

These memoirs of the gentle "Elia" are full of instruction and interest; his life-devotion to his afflicted sister is sufficient to stamp his character with the truest heroism. No writer, perhaps, appeals more to the sympathies of his readers, and the quaintness which shows itself in the most unimportant of his letters renders them truly delightful reading.

Campbell, Lord. Lives of the Lord Chancellors of England (2).

——— *Lives of the Lord Chief Justices of England* (2).

These are the biographies of men eminent in the law for many generations, painted not unworthily by a sympathizer, and yet with reasonable fairness and impartiality.—*Ch. King.*

Walpole, Horace. Memoirs and Correspondence.

Delightful reading.—*Ch. King.*

Carlyle, Thos. Letters and Speeches of Oliver Cromwell.
Ch. King.

Russell, Lord John. Life and Times of Lord William Russell.—Ch. King.

Vansantavoord, G. Life of Algeron Sydney.
Ch. King.

Nugent, Lord. Memorials of John Hampden.
Ch. King.

Guizot. Life of General Monk, Duke of Albemarle (1).
Ch. King.

Brydges, Sir Edgerton. Autobiography.

Curious and full of interest.

Moore, Thomas. Life and Letters of Lord Byron.

——— *Life and Death of Lord Edward Fitzgerald.*

Milton, John. A Biography.
By Cyrus R. Edwards.

Ivimey, Jos. Life and Times of John Milton.

A clear and succinct history of the life of the "Blind Bard," and worthy of perusal from its general historical interest.

King, Lord. Life of John Locke.

The life of England's most renowned philosopher.

Northcote's Life of Sir Joshua Reynolds.

Ch. King.

Brougham, Lord. Lives of Men of Letters and Science of the Times of George III. (1).—*Ch. King.*

Kelly's Reminiscences of the Stage.

An entertaining volume.—*Ch. King.*

Dix. Life of Chatterton.

A history of the life of the "remarkable boy," whose truly great genius, under proper guidance, would have placed him among the first of England's poets.

Carlyle. Life of Sterling (2).

A charming biography, written with all the freedom and vigor which characterized the earlier works of Carlyle.

Wordsworth, William. Biography.

By Dr. CHRISTOPHER WORDSWORTH.

Interesting, though somewhat labored. It is ably edited in the American edition by Prof. Henry Reed.

Campbell, Thomas. Life and Letters.

Edited by WILLIAM BEATTIE.

These volumes do not render justice to the poet, the editor being but indifferently qualified for his task. Yet they may be perused with advantage, as giving much valuable information of the private life of a popular poet.

Southey. Life and Correspondence (1).

Biographies of literary men are ever interesting, and the present one affords a remarkable evidence of the industry with which Southey devoted himself to the pursuit of literature, and should especially be read by young men as being most worthy of imitation.

Keats. Life and Letters.
Edited by R. M. Milnes.

An affectionate tribute to the memory of a sensitive genius.

Goëthe. Autobiography (1).
Translated by Parke Godwin.

Brewster, Sir David. Lives of the Martyrs of Science.
(Galileo, Tycho Brahe, and Kepler.)

Benvenuto Cellini. Memoirs.
'By himself.

The life of a son of Genius, unregulated, varied, fierce, and in these present times almost incredible.—*Ch. King.*

Dumont, E. Recollections of Mirabeau.

Apocryphal, possibly, in some of its statements, especially as to the part which Dumont professes to have had in suggesting some of the most eloquent of the brilliant speeches of the demagogue, yet very interesting in the portraiture of an unprincipled man of genius, by an intimate friend.—*Ch. King.*

Pellico, Silvio. My Prisons (1).

A work which cannot be read without a rising of the heart against the wanton and refined cruelty of Austrian oppression.—*Ch. King.*

Lee, Mrs. Old Painters.

This is a delightful book, especially for the young. It is full of taste and right feeling, and contains instruction for the heart as well as head.—*Bp. Potter.*

Barrow. Life of Peter the Great (1).

The life of one of the most extraordinary characters that ever appeared on the great theatre of the world in any age or country.—*Preface to Work.*

Dyer. Life of Calvin (1).

A full, earnest, and interesting memoir of the great champion of Protestantism, worthy of careful reading.

Lee, Mrs. Life of Martin Luther (1).

Graphic, picturesque, and with few exceptions just.—*Bp. Potter.*

Roscoe. Life of Cervantes (1).

An interesting sketch of the life of the world-renowned author of Don Quixotte.

Buxton, Charles. Memoirs of Sir Tho's Fowell Buxton.

Dixon. Life of William Penn.

Prescott's Ferdinand and Isabella (1).

Hanna, Dr. Life of Thomas Chalmers (1).

Southey's Life of Wesley (1).

IV.

TRAVELS.

I. UNITED STATES.

Carver's Travels, 1766–1768 (3).

These travels excited much attention soon after the Revolutionary war. He commenced his travels, as he stated, from Michilimackinac, which was then regarded as far beyond the verge of the civilized world; and he traversed the (now) State of Wisconsin to the Mississippi.—*Kent.*

La Rochefoucald-Liancourt. Travels in the United States in 1795.

Brissott de Warville. Travels in the United States in 1780.

Chastelleux. Travels in the United States in 1780 (3).

These three French travellers, much read in former days, are now seldom referred to; yet if only for comparison of the past and the present, their pages will be found interesting and their tone friendly.—*Ch. King.*

Henry's Travels and Adventures in Canada and the Indian Territories, between 1760 *and* 1776 (2).

He was among the prisoners taken at the capture of Michilimackinac by the Indians, in June, 1763; and after his release he went to the northwest regions as far as Cumberland House, and there found a British garrison of Highlanders from the Orkney Islands! His enterprise, perils, and intrepidity, excite deep interest.—*Kent.*

Lewis and Clark's Expedition up the Missouri and across the Rocky Mountains, to the Columbia River, in 1804 *and* 1805 (2).

Was under the direction of the government of the United States, and ably executed.—*Kent.*

Pike's Expeditions to the Sources of the Mississippi and of the Arkansas, in 1805, '6, '7 (2).

Was another government equipment, and performed with energy.—*Kent.*

Irving's Astoria.

——— *Captain Bonneville's Adventures in the Far West* (1).

These volumes are full of exciting incident, and by reason of Mr. Irving's fine taste and attractive style, they possess the power and the charms of romance.—*Kent.*

Long's Expedition from Pittsburgh to the Rocky Mountains, in 1819 *and* 1820 (2).

And his Second Expedition to the source of St. Peter's River, in 1823, under the orders of the government of the United States, reflected credit on the power that planned, and on the agents who carried it into execution.—*Kent.*

Schoolcraft's Travels from Detroit to the Sources of the Mississippi, in 1820 (2).

And his travels to the central portions of the Mississippi Valley, in 1821, and his travels through the Upper Mississippi to the Itascä Lake, in 1832 (2), were all government expeditions, and the details are very interesting.—*Kent.*

Parker's Exploring Tour beyond the Rocky Mountains, in 1838 (2).

This is one of the most authentic and interesting accounts we have of the country of Oregon or waters of the Columbia, and of the character of the

Indian tribes in that savage country. The author brings to the subject all the knowledge, industry, candor, and piety, becoming his mission and pretensions.—*Kent.*

Fearon. Narrative of a Journey of 5,000 *Miles through the Eastern and Western States, in* 1817 (2).

Hodgson, Adam A. Journey through North America in 1819–1821 (2).

Hamilton, Thomas. Men and Manners in America (3).

Buckingham, J. S. Travels in America (2).

Hall, Basil. Travels in America in 1827–8 (3).

Murray, C. A. Travels in America in 1839 (1).

Marryatt. Diary in America (3).

Dickens. American Notes for General Circulation (3).

Here are grouped a series of English travellers, the perusal of whose pages may not be unprofitable. Exaggerated and absurd as are some of the censures, and fault-finding to our somewhat overweening self-esteem, the lesson will not be lost if it lead us to look at home, and not abroad, for our opinions, not less than our manners, habits, and fabrics.—*Ch. King.*

Pike, Z. M. Travels to the Sources of Western Rivers (2).

Flint. Recollections of Ten Years in the Valley of the Mississippi (2).

These chronicles profess marvellously, yet their marvels are left far behind, by those now passing under our own eyes.—*Ch. King.*

Lyell, Sir Charles. Travels in North America in 1841–2 (1).

—— ———— *Second Visit to the United States* (1).

Wortley, Lady Stuart. Visit to the United States (2).

These publications prove, that the more refined and intelligent the traveller among us, the less cause is found for annoyance and complaint; proving that vulgar assumption, and ignorant presumption provoke more probably the inconveniences so pathetically or ridiculously chronicled by the Fearons, Halls, and Hamiltons.—*Ch. King.*

Colton, Walter. Three Years in California (2).

Greenhow. Oregon and California (2).

Fremont. Narrative of an Exploring Expedition to the Rocky Mountains (1).

Emory. Reconnoissance of New Mexico (2).

Taylor, Bayard. El Dorado, or Adventures in the Paths of Empire (2).

Should all be read; for now these once far-off regions have become to us as household words.

Kendall, George W. The Santa Fé Expedition (1).

A narrative of strange adventure and daring, of American recklessness, and of Mexican inefficiency and cruelty.

Hoffman, C. F. Winter in the West (2).

Schultz's Travels on an Inland Voyage from Albany to New-Orleans in 1807 *and* 1808 (3).

This work affords an incontestable proof of the rapid and astonishing improvement in internal communication and commerce within the last thirty years, by means of canals, steamboats, and railroads; and of the great difficulty and peril of transportation, at that era, up the Mohawk, and down the Wood Creek and Oneida Lake to Oswego, and from thence to Niagara and Buffalo, and from Presque Isle to Pittsburgh; and then in barges and Kentucky boats down the Ohio and dangerous Mississippi to New-Orleans.—*Kent*, 1840.

Agassiz. Tour on Lake Superior (2).

A very intelligent and interesting sketch of travels in a region which is as yet comparatively unknown.

Butler (Mrs. Fanny Kemble). Journal in America (3).

Ruxton, G. F. Life in the Far West (2).

Parkman, Francis, Jr. California and Oregon Trail (1).

The last a sparkling book of adventures, and full of interest and information.

Texas—A Visit to it in 1831 (2).
Kent.

Parker. Trip to Texas in 1834, 35 (2).
Kent.

II. OTHER PARTS OF AMERICA.

Charlevoix's Travels in Canada, from Quebec to New-Orleans in 1720 (3).

This is the most valuable of all his works. He was a Jesuit, and a learned and pious man, of great simplicity and integrity. See also Hearne's Journey from Hudson's Bay to the mouth of Copper Mine River, in 1771. He was the first white man that discovered the Northern Ocean west of Baffin's Bay, and east of Behring's Straits.—*Kent.*

Head, Sir F. B. Forest Scenes, &c., in Canada (1).

McKenzie's Voyages from Montreal to the Frozen and Pacific Oceans, in 1789 *and* 1793 (3).—*Kent.*

Latrobe's Rambler in Mexico, in 1834 (2).
Kent.

Poinsett's Travels to, and Notes on, Mexico, in 1822 (2).
Kent.

Barca, Mad. Calderon de la. Life in Mexico (2).

Mayer, Brantz. Mexico as it Was, and as it Is (2).

Thompson, Waddy. Recollections of Mexico (2).

Ruxton, Geo. F. Adventures in Mexico and the Rocky Mountains (2).

These publications, contrasted with the Notes on Mexico, by Mr. Poinsett, in 1822, present a picture of the unprogressive condition of society in Mexico. The next epoch of twenty years subsequent to the late war between our country and Mexico, will show far other results. The last author named above is an Englishman, who saw little or nothing to admire in Mexico but the scenery.—*Ch. King.*

Humboldt's Travels to the Equatorial Regions (1).
Kent.

Thompson's Official Visit to Guatemala, in 1825 (2).
Kent.

Dunn's Residence in Central America, 1827 (2).
Kent.

Terry's Travels to the Equatorial Regions, in 1832 (2).
Kent.

Notes on a Journey from Caraccas to Bogota (2).
By an Officer of the United States, in 1822.—*Kent.*

Depont's Voyage to Terra Firma, in 1801–4 (3).

This work was deemed very valuable at the time of its publication, but in this very revolutionary age and temper of mankind, all travels and geography become comparatively obsolete in thirty years. Such is the impatient and restless spirit of the times, that nothing seems to be very palatable that is not very new.—*Kent.*

Ulloa's Voyages to South America, 1735–1746 (2).

Admirable. They contain a picture of Peru *as it was*, before the violence of earthquakes, and the tenfold more violent passions of man had consigned it to desolation.—*Kent.*

Walsh's Notices of Brazil, in 1829 (2).

Caldclough's Travels in South America, in 1819–1821 (2).
Kent.

Warren, J. E. Para, or Scenes of Adventures on the Amazon (2).

Para is styled the Paradise of Brazil, and yet is rarely visited, and more rarely described.—*Ch. King.*

Stephens, J. L. Incidents of Travel in Central America, Chipias, and Yucatan (1).

——— *Incidents of Travel in Yucatan* (1).

Mr. Stephens's books possess great interest, giving a copious description of those mysterious relics of the early possessors of the American continent, which have never hitherto excited their due share of interest.—*London Athenæum.*

Norman, B. M. Ruined Cities of Yucatan (2).

Valuable for the many drawings of important ruins, and of the first collection of idols ever discovered, which are extremely curious and unique.—*London Athenæum.*

Squier, E. G. The Serpent Symbol (3).

——— ——— *Nicaragua, its People, &c.* (2).

These two works will give the reader a full and reliable account of this most interesting portion of our continent, prepared by a graceful, animated, and spirited writer, who possessed superior advantages of observation and information. The plates illustrating the volumes will give much valuable information as to the numerous relics of antiquity, with which Central America abounds.

Tschudi, Von, Dr. J. S. Travels in Peru in 1838–1842 (2). Translated from the German by J. Thomasina Ross.

Bigelow, John. Jamaica in 1850 (2).

III. EUROPE GENERALLY.

Dewey, Orville. Old World and New (2).

Haight, Mrs. Letters from the Old World (2).

Mitchell, D. G. (Ik Marvel). Fresh Gleanings (2).

Slidell's American in Spain (2).

——— *Spain Revisited* (2).

Colman, Henry. European Life and Manners (2).

Ware, Wm. European Capitals (2).

Sedgwick, Miss. Letters from Abroad (1).

Kirkland, Mrs. C. M. Holidays Abroad, or Europe from the West (2).

Taylor, Bayard. Views-a-Foot (1).

Are all excellent works, and worthy of attention, as being the views of intelligent American travellers upon the manners, customs, and society of the Old World.

IV. GREAT BRITAIN.

The British Tourist, by Mavor, 1798 (3).

This is a valuable collection. It includes some of the best travels in Great Britain, such as those of Johnson, Boswell, Pennant, Young, Hutchinson, Newte, &c. See also Lettice's Tour through Scotland, in 1792, and Sir Walter Scott's Visit to the Shetland Islands, in 1812, embodied in Lockhart's Life of Scott.—*Kent.*

Silliman. Journal in 1805, 6 (3).

Simond. Tour and Residence in Great Britain in 1810, 11 (2).—*Ch. King.*

Wheaton. Journal of a Residence in England in 1823, 24 (3).

Carter. Letters from Europe, 1825 (2).

Colton. Four Years' Residence in Great Britain in 1831--35 (1).

Stewart. Sketches of Society in 1832 (2).

Allen. Practical Tourist in 1832 (2).

Humphrey. Great Britain, France, and Belgium, 1835 (2).

Slidell. Young American in England, 1835 (2).

Sedgwick. Letters from Abroad to Kindred at Home (1).

Olmsted. Walks and Talks of an American Farmer in England (1).

Are all by American travellers. They contain sketches of society and manners, and are all written with purity and good taste. Allen's Practical Tourist contains the richest fund of practical and useful observation.

Lester, C. Edwards. The Glory and Shame of England (2).

——— ——— *The Condition and Fate of England* (2).

Bulwer, E. L. England and the English (2).

Carlyle, Thos. Past and Present (1).

Rush, Richard. Residence at the Court of London (2).
Ch. King.

Sinclair, Miss. Scotland and the Scotch (1).

Written in a piquant, lively style, and evidencing the writer to be a lady of fine talents and much observation.

Thackeray, W. M. Irish Sketch Book (1).

A pleasant book of travels, full of interest to the general reader, and of many curious sketches of this singular people.

Howitt, William. Rural Life in England (1).

The best of William Howitt's works in this department. He always writes with spirit, and in a kindly tone; but his opinions are of less value than his descriptions.—*Bp. Potter.*

V. FRANCE.

Young's Travels in France, 1787–9 (3).
Kent.

Carter's Letters from Europe, 1825 (2).
Kent.

Moore's Views of Society in France in 1773, '4 (3).
Kent.

Moore's Journal of a Residence in France in 1792 (3).
Kent.

Humphrey's Great Britain, France, &c. (2).
Kent.

Sanderson, John. American in Paris (2).

Janin, Jules. American in Paris during the Summer (2).

—— *American in Paris during the Winter* (2).

Mitchell, D. G. (Ik Marvel). Battle Summer (2).

Trollope, Mrs. Paris and the Parisians in 1835 (3).

Anthon, Chas. E. Pilgrimage to Treves in 1844 (2).

Bulwer, H. L. France—Social, Political, and Literary (2).

VI. SPAIN AND PORTUGAL.

Swinburne's Travels in Spain, in 1775 *and* 1776 (3).
Kent.

Young's Travels in Catalonia (2).
Kent.

Bourgoanne's Travels in Spain (3).

He resided in Spain eighteen years.—*Kent.*

Townsend's Journey in Spain, in 1786 *and* 1787 (3).

All these travels over Spain were prior to the French Revolution, and they are all of high character and value. Since the commencement of that period, Spain has been the theatre of ferocious wars, and the physical and moral resources of the kingdom and the character of the people amply tested and delineated in the military history of that country.—*Kent.*

Mackenzie, Alex. Slidell. Year in Spain (1).

——— *Spain Revisited* (1).

Irving, Washington. The Alhambra (1).

A series of charming sketches, interspersed with the legends connected with this ancient palace of the Moorish dynasty in Spain, full to the brim of interest.

Ford, Richard. Spaniards and their Country (1).

A careful and judicious work, and worthy of confidence.

Warren, J. E. Vagamundo; or, The Attaché in Spain (2).

A racy, readable sketch of life in Spain at the present day.

Chaulet's Travels in Portugal (3).
(From the French.)

Hughes, T. M. Overland Journey to Lisbon in 1846 (3).

Borrow, George. Bible in Spain (1).

——— *Zincali; or, The Gipsies in Spain* (1).

Should be read by every one; they are the production of a close observer and clever writer.

VII. ITALY AND SICILY.

Moore's View of Society in Italy, 1776 (3).
Kent.

Eustace's Classical Tour in Italy, 1802 (2).
Kent.

Forsyth on Italy, 1802 *and* 1803 (2).
Kent.

Swinburne's Travels in the Kingdom of Naples and Sicily, 1777–1780 (2).—*Kent.*

Brydone's Tour in Sicily and Malta in 1770 (2).

Italy has been inundated with a host of travellers; those that have been selected are among the most interesting; they are highly valuable and instructive. Those of Eustace and Swinburne evince great classical erudition, criticism, and taste.—*Kent.*

Of more modern travellers, the following are deemed the most worthy of confidence:—

Turnbull, Rev. Robert. Genius of Italy (1).

Tuckerman, H. T. The Italian Sketch-Book (2).

——— *Sicily: a Pilgrimage* (1).

The last two works, the production of one of our own gifted Literateurs, are especially commended to the kind attention of the student. They are well written, and are full of beauties and information.

Mariotti, L. Italy, Past and Present (2).

Pompeii (1).
2 vols. London, 1836.

Kip, W. I. Christmas Holidays in Rome (1).

VIII. HOLLAND, BELGIUM, GERMANY, AND SWITZERLAND.

Johnson, Dr. J. Excursions through France, Belgium, Germany, Switzerland, and Italy (3).

Excellent.—*Kent.*

Coxe's Travels in Switzerland (2).
Published in London, in 1789.

They give the most thorough examination of that most picturesque and romantic of all civilized countries.—*Kent.*

Cooper, J. F. Travels in Switzerland (2).

They are fair, liberal, and truly and graphically descriptive.—*Kent.*

Agassiz. Journey to, and Tours in Switzerland (2).

Anderson, Hans Christian. Rambles in the Hartz Mountains (2). From the Danish.

Inglis, H. D. The Tyrol, with a Glance at Bavaria (2).

Cheever, Geo. B. Wanderings of a Pilgrim in the Shadow of the Jungfrau Alps* (2).

Moore's View of Society in Germany and Switzerland, 1775 *and* 1776 (3).—*Kent.*

Russell's Travels in Germany and Austria, 1820–22 (3).

They have deservedly a very high reputation.—*Kent.*

Montague, Lady. Travels through Germany and Hungary to Constantinople, in 1716 *and* 1717 (2).

They are written with great vivacity and elegance.—*Kent.*

Dwight's Travels in the North of Germany, 1825 *and* 1826 (2).—*Kent.*

Walsh's Journey from Constantinople to Vienna in 1827 (2).—*Kent.*

Howitt, Wm. Student Life in Germany (2).

—— *Rural and Domestic Life in Germany* (2).

Witling, H. J. Heidelberg, and the Way thither (2).

—— *Nuremberg and its Vicinity* (2).

Kohl, J. G. Travels in Austria (2).

Staël, Madame de. Germany (2).

This work is rich in acute and ingenious ideas, but has been justly criticised as containing many erroneous views. Her taste is not altogether correct, her style is irregular and has too much pretension, but in all her works we find originality and profound thought, great acuteness, a lively imagination, a philosophical insight into the human heart and into the truths of politics and literature.—*Enc. Am.*

Tour through Holland in 1828 (2).
Kent.

Simpson's and Scott's Visits to Belgium and Waterloo in 1815 (2).—*Kent.*

IX. NORTH OF EUROPE.

Coxe. Travels in Poland, Russia, Sweden, and Denmark (2).
This work abounds in historical and biographical details.—*Kent.*

Acerbi's Travels from Stockholm to the North Cape, in 1798 *and* 1799 (3).—*Kent.*

Clarke's Travels in Sweden and Russia, as well as in Asia Minor, Palestine, and Greece, in 1800 *and* 1801 (2).

Erman's Travels in Siberia (1).

Kohl, J. G. Russia and the Russians (1).

Thompson, E. P. Life in Russia (2).

Elliott's Travels in Sweden and Norway, 1830 (3).
Kent.

Laing's Residence in Norway, in 1834, '35, *and* '36 (2).
Kent.

Foster. Norway in 1849 (2).

Laing's Tour in Sweden in 1838 (2).
Kent.

Ida Pfeiffer's Journey to Iceland.
Translated by Miss Cooper.

Mackenzie, Sir G. Travels in Iceland, 1810 (3).
Kent.

Henderson's Missionary Tour in Iceland, in 1814, '15 (2). *Kent.*

Jermann. Pictures from St. Petersburg (1).

Maxwell. The Czar, his Court and People (2).

Standish's Notices of the Northern Capitals, 1838 (3).

Stephens's Incidents of Travel in Greece, Turkey, Russia, and Poland, in 1835 (1).—*Kent.*

Murray. Hand-Book for Northern Europe (1).

X. WESTERN ASIA.

Clarke's Travels in Palestine, in connection with Egypt, Greece, and the North of Europe (2).—*Kent.*

Volney's Travels through Syria and Egypt, 1783–85 (3).

They are distinguished for intelligence and accuracy.—*Kent.*

Niebuhr's Travels in Arabia, 1761–67 (2).

They maintain the highest reputation for accuracy and fulness of research. —*Kent.*

Burckhardt's Travels in Nubia, 1813 (2). *Kent.*

——— *Travels in Arabia,* 1814 (2).

He was intrepid and accomplished as a traveller in Mahometan countries. —*Kent.*

Morier's Journey through Persia, Armenia, and Asia Minor, in 1808 *and* 1809, *in a Diplomatic Character* (2).—*Kent.*

Kepple's Travels in Babylonia, Media, Georgia, and Astracan, in 1824 (2).—*Kent.*

Laborde's Journey to Mount Sinai and Petrea, in 1828 (2). *Kent.*

Stephens's Incidents of Travel in Egypt, Arabia and Petrea, and the Holy Land, in 1836 (1).—*Kent.*

Addison's Journey from Malta to Greece, Constantinople, Smyrna, Rhodes, Syria, Damascus, and Palmyra, in 1835 (2).

This last work is written with singular judgment, elegance, and taste.—*Kent.*

Smith and Dwight's Researches in Armenia, 1830, '31 (2).

Exceedingly instructive.—*Kent.*

Jones's Excursions to Egypt and Syria, in 1834 (2). *Kent.*

Wilbraham's Travels in Georgia and Caucasian Russia, in 1837 (2).

This traveller is distinguished for crossing and recrossing the snowy Caucasus.—*Kent.*

Crosby, Howard. The Land of the Moslem (2).

Madden, R. Travels in Turkey and Egypt (2).

Macfarlane, C. Turkey and its Destiny (2).

Layard, A. H. Nineveh and its Remains (1).

One of the most interesting works of the present day, and which cannot be too warmly recommended. The buried cities of the East have ever been among the marvels of the world—they promise not to be so much longer.

Lindsay's Letters on Egypt, Edom, and the Holy Land (1).

I do not know of a collection of books of travels better calculated to command the attention, exercise the sympathies, and gratify the curiosity and taste of the reader, than those here enumerated on Western Asia.—*Kent.*

Curzon, Rob't. Visit to the Monasteries of the Levant (1).

Warburton, Eliot. Crescent and the Cross (1).

Kinglake. Eothen; or, Traces of Eastern Travel (2).

Three most charming works of travels, written with good taste and excellent judgment. The first is full of curious information for the lover of antiquarian lore.—*Ch. King.*

Olin, Rev. S. Travels in Egypt, Arabia, Petrea, &c. (2).

Spencer. The East; or, Travels in Egypt and the Holy Land (1).

Robinson, Edw., D. D. Biblical Researches in Palestine in 1838 (2).

Southgate, Rev. H., D. D. Narrative of a Tour through Armenia, Kurdistan, Persia, &c. (2).

Chateaubriand's Travels in Greece, Palestine, and Egypt, in 1806 *and* 1807 (2). Translated by SHOBERL. And

Lamartine's Travels in the East, in 1832, '33 (2).

Are equally charged as being romantic and of a legendary cast; but they are most fascinating books, adorned with taste, elegance, and learning, and full of the descriptive and pathetic eloquence, which the fire of genius and the ardor of Christian enthusiasm inspire.—*Kent.*

Lynch, W. F. Dead Sea Expedition (1).

A narrative of much interest, of the expedition fitted out by the United States government for the exploration of this singular sea, which has defied the efforts of the world of science to resolve.

Wainwright's Pathways and Abiding Places of our Lord (2).

——— *Land of Bondage* (2).

XI. EASTERN ASIA AND THE PACIFIC ISLANDS.

Elphinstone's Embassy from Delhi in India to Cabul, in 1808 (3).

This was a diplomatic embassy from the British East India government, and gives a very specific and authentic account of the Afghan tribes and empire.—*Kent.*

Burnes's Travels in Upper India, and through the Snowy Range of the Hindoo Koosh or Himalayah Mountains to Bokhara; and a Passage also up the Indus in 1831–33 (3).—*Kent.*

Bishop Heber's Journeys through the Upper and Southern Provinces of India, in 1824, '5, '6 (2).—*Kent.*

Simmes's Public Embassy to the Capital of the Birman Empire, in 1795 (3).—*Kent.*

Malcolm's Missionary Travels in South-Eastern Asia, in 1835, '36 (2).—*Kent.*

Bell's Travels in 1720, *from Petersburgh to Pekin* (3). *Kent.*

Lord Macartney's Embassy to China, 1792, '3, '4 (2). By Stanton.—*Kent.*

Barrow's Travels in China, as attached to the same Embassy (3).—*Kent.*

Lord Amherst's Embassy to China, 1816 (3). By Ellis.

These four last productions give us the best account, by intelligent and sagacious observers, of the manners and customs, and arts and learning, of a mean and semi-barbarous race, without any due sense of the obligations of humanity, justice, or truth.—*Kent.*

Roberts, E. Embassy to China in the Peacock, 1832–4 (3).

Williams, S. W. The Chinese Empire (1).

Ellis, Henry. Journal of an Embassy from England to China, in 1816 (2).

Crawford, John. Journal of an Embassy from India to Siam and China (2).

Burnes, Sir Alex. Residence in Cabool, 1836–38 (1).

Brooke, J. Narrative of Events in Borneo (1).

Forbes, F. E. Five Years in China, 1842–47 (1).

Arrian's Expedition of Alexander in India (2).
Translated by J. Rooke.

The conquests and annexations now in progress by the English in India, extending over the fields of Alexander's marches and victories, lend a new and present interest to this old work.—*Ch. King.*

Oxley's Expeditions into the Interior of New South Wales, in 1817 *and* 1818 (3).—*Kent.*

Mitchell's Expeditions into the same, 1831 *and* 1835 (3). *Kent.*

Leigh's Travels in South Australia, in 1836 (2).

These three last works, and particularly the two first, are wonderfully well calculated to excite and gratify intense curiosity, as to the hidden recesses, and solitudes, and deserts, of a mighty and mysterious continent.—*Kent.*

Cheever, H. T. The Sandwich Islands (2).

Stewart, C. J. Residence in Sandwich Islands (1).

Simpson, Alex. The Sandwich Islands since their Discovery and Occupation (2).

Macaulay, W. H. Kathay: a Cruise in the China Seas.

Melville. Typee (2). *Omoo* (2).

Very attractive books of adventure, but rather too much tinged with the marvellous and romantic, to give them any character as reliable works.

Colton, W. Deck and Port: a Cruise to California (3).

XII. · AFRICA.

Volney's Travels through Syria and Egypt (3).

Mentioned already.—*Kent.*

Savary's Letters on Egypt, 1777 (2).

Beautifully and eloquently written, but too glowing and exaggerated.—*Kent.*

Leigh's Narrative of a Journey up the Nile into Nubia, in 1813 (2).—*Kent.*

Travels of Ali Bey, in 1803–1807, *in Morocco, Egypt, Arabia, and Syria* (3).

The real traveller was Badia, a Spaniard; and he had the requisite accomplishments for the purpose.—*Kent.*

Denon's Travels in Egypt with the French Army (2).

Published originally in Paris, in 1802.

They were ushered into the world with great expense and magnificence, but are regarded as comparatively light and flippant. His relation of a visit by moonlight to the mouth of the Nile soon after Nelson's great victory, when the shores were covered with wrecks of the battle, and the bodies of the wretched victims, is eloquent, picturesque, and awful in the highest degree. —*Kent.*

Bruce's Travels in Egypt, Nubia, and Abyssinia, to discover the Sources of the Nile, in 1768–73 (2).

The first and last, and especially the latter, are very interesting. He was an intrepid and faithful traveller, and modern writers of the first authority bear testimony to his general accuracy. Sir William Jones said, that Bruce gave more accurate information concerning the nations from the fountains to the mouth of the Nile, than all Europe could have supplied. The discovery of the head of the Nile was a great point among the ancients; and Julius Cæsar, according to Lucan, was willing to abandon all his ambitious projects, if he could thereby be enabled to make the discovery.—*Kent.*

Hawks, Rev. F. L. Monuments of Egypt; or, Egypt a Witness for the Bible (1).

Furniss. Waraga; or, Charms of the Nile (2).

Curtis, G. W. Nile Notes of a Howadji (2).

Brown, W. G. Travels to Dar-Fur, 1792–98 (2).

To discover the head of White River, or the western branch of the Nile, as Bruce only followed up the eastern branch to its source. Brown was an excellent and extraordinary character.—*Kent.*

Werne, Fred. Expedition to the White Nile, 1840, '41 (2). From the German.

Salt's Travels in Abyssinia, in 1809, '10 (2).

He went in the capacity of a public agent, and his travels are evidence of his judgment and scholarship. He was well received, and found some interesting vestiges of Christian faith and worship among a turbulent and savage people.—*Kent.*

Russell's Nubia and Abyssinia (1).

Kent.

Lane's Modern Egyptians (1).

All the accounts of Egypt are worth studying. That singular country has arrested the attention of mankind from the earliest records of sacred and profane history. The valley of the Nile is of exuberant and matchless fertility, though it is hemmed in on each side by frightful deserts. The malediction of heaven seems to have attended Egypt from the time of the Pharaohs. It has excited the cupidity, and been the prey of conquerors and tyrants, for three thousand years. Its present condition is deplorable, under the stern administration of the most vigorous and remorseless of despots.—*Kent.*

Park's Travels into the Interior of Africa, 1795, '6, '7 (2).

Kent.

Park's Travels into the same, in 1805 (2).

Kent.

Denham and Clapperton's Travels in Central Africa, in 1822, '23, '24 (2).—*Kent.*

Clapperton and Lander's in the same, in 1826 (2). *Kent.*

Laird and Oldfield's Voyage into the same by Steam-vessels, in 1832, '3, '4 (2).—*Kent.*

Lempriere's Tour through the Kingdom of Morocco, in 1790 (3).—*Kent.*

Lamping (Clemens) and M. de Vauce. The French in Algiers (2). From the French and German.

Tuckey, Capt. Expedition up the River Zaire, in 1816 (2). *Kent.*

Morrell, Capt. Third Voyage, containing Excursions into Western Africa, 1828, '29 (2).—*Kent.*

Allen. Expedition to the Niger, 1831 (2).

Pringle, Thos. Residence in South Africa (2).

Vaillant's Travels in South Africa, in 1783, '4, '5 (3). *Kent.*

Barrow's Travels in South Africa, 1797, '98 (3).

This was official and very accurate.—*Kent.*

Kay's Missionary Travels in Caffraria, in 1825, '26 (2). *Kent.*

Alexander's Expedition into the Interior of South Africa, 1836, '37 (2).—*Kent.*

Harris's Sporting Voyage into the same, 1836 (2).

The various travellers into Central and Southern Africa have excited a deep interest in the civilized world, but with the exception of the feeble settlement of Liberia, very little impression seems to have been made upon the numerous tribes of barbarians who inhabit the vast and unknown interior of that continent. The boundaries of the colony at the Cape of Good Hope are checked by fierce savages, and we are indebted to the few humble stations of the missionaries, for the only vestiges of Christianity and civilization which exist out of the colony, to cheer, like so many oases, the surrounding deserts. —*Kent.*

Forbes, Fred. E. Dahomey and the Dahomeans (2).

V.

VOYAGES.

I. THE SOUTH PACIFIC, AND AROUND THE WORLD.

The early *Spanish* and *Portuguese* voyages to the South Sea and round the world by Magellan, Sebastian Cano, Garcia de Loyosa, Sarvedra, Ulloa, Mendoza, Quivos, Garcia de Nodal; and the early *English* voyages to the South Sea and round the globe by Drake, Cavendish, Sir John Hawkins, Sir John Narborough, Dampier, Cowley, Rogers, and Clipperton; and the early *Dutch* voyages to the South Sea by Spilberg, La Maire, Schouten, Le Hermite, Tasman, Vlaming, and Roggewein, are all narrated in *Callender's Voyages to the Terra-Australis*, 3 vols., Edin., 1767. Many of the voyages are excellently well narrated, and are full of exciting interest, and discover great enterprise, daring, skill, and judgment. The early voyages to the South Sea, and the early circumnavigators of the globe, are also well detailed in *Harpers' Family Library*, No. 30 and No. 82. See also *Burney's History* of the discoveries in the Pacific Ocean, from 1579 to 1723, 4 vols., 4to.—*Kent.*

Anson's Voyage, 1740–44.

This work is elegantly written, and was, during the last generation, the most popular nautical production that had ever been written. Before Byron's voyage the great South Sea was regarded as one vast solitary ocean, without island or shelter, except the two small islands of *Juan Fernandez* and *Tinian* at each side of the Pacific, where Anson refreshed his exhausted crews. Each of them was regarded as a terrestrial paradise, planted there by Providence to alleviate the distresses and dangers incident to the navigation of that ocean.—*Kent.*

Hawkesworth's Voyages; consisting of

1. *Byron's Voyage, in* 1764;
2. *Wallis's Voyage, in* 1766;
3. *Carteret's Voyage,* 1766;
4. *Cook's First Voyage,* 1768–1771.—*Kent.*

Bourgainville's Voyage, 1766–69.
Kent.

Cook's Second Voyage, 1772–75.
Kent.

—— *Third Voyage,* 1776–80.

This last voyage was one of the most interesting and valuable. The introduction by Dr. Douglass, afterwards Bishop of Salisbury, has been greatly admired.—*Kent.*

La Perouse's Voyage, 1785–88.

One of the most unfortunate of all the efforts at nautical discovery, and awakens the deepest sympathy.—*Kent.*

Vancouver's Voyage of Discovery in the North Pacific. 1791–95.

This great voyage was performed with admirable skill, discipline, perseverance, and success.—*Kent.*

Wilson's Missionary Voyage, 1796–98.
Kent.

Trumbull's Voyage, 1800–1804.
Kent.

Porter's Cruise in the Pacific, 1812–14.
Kent.

Tyerman and Bennet's Missionary Voyages, 1821–29.
Kent.

Beechy's Voyage to the Pacific, 1825–28.

This was a voyage under the orders of the British government, to co-operate with the Polar Expeditions beyond Behring's Strait.—*Kent.*

Wilkes, Capt. The United States' Exploring Expedition, 1838–42 (1). In 5 vols., and also an abridgment in 1 vol.

Ruschenburg, Dr. Three Years in the Pacific, in 1833 (1).

Olmsted, F. A. Incidents of a Whaling Voyage, with Notices of the Sandwich Islands (1).

The Pacific, to which these works relate, and which may now, according to the Roman usage, almost be called *mare nostrum*, cannot be too much studied.—*Ch. King.*

Reynold's Voyage in the Frigate Potomac, around the Globe, 1831–34.—*Kent.*

King and Fitzroy, Captains. Surveying Voyages on the Coasts of South America, 1826–36.

It would be difficult to point out any course of reading relative to the active concerns of mankind, better calculated to amuse and instruct the reader, than the series of voyages that have been mentioned. The management of those little communities, the ships with their crews, brings into view the noblest endowments of the mind and heart. Such voyages have peril and incident, sufficient to keep curiosity, joy, and sympathy, in perpetual action. They enlarge, with wonderful facility and dispatch, our knowledge of the globe and its physical phenomena, its vegetable and animal productions, and they exhibit living pictures of human nature in all its shades of rudeness and barbarity. They enkindle a disposition and zeal to cultivate intercourse and trade with new and distant nations; to introduce among them the useful arts, and to make them acquainted with the social and religious institutions of civilized life.—*Kent.*

Mutiny of the Bounty.

A description of Pitcairn's Island and its inhabitants, with an account of the mutiny and subsequent fortunes of the mutineers.

Waddell's Voyage towards the South Pole, 1822–24.

This was a private trading voyage. Captain Waddell penetrated the antarctic sea to latitude 74, which was three degrees further south than Cook or any preceding navigator had penetrated.—*Kent.*

Morrell's Voyages in the Southern Hemisphere, in America, Africa, and Asia, between 1822 *and* 1831.

These were private trading voyages, but performed with admirable skill, and with enthusiastic spirit and enterprise.—*Kent.*

Owen's Voyages to the Coasts of Southern Africa and Madagascar, 1823–26.

They were skilfully and resolutely executed, under great peril and deplorable sickness, along the most sickly and hateful of shores.—*Kent.*

Stewart's Voyage as a Missionary to the Sandwich Islands, 1823–25.—*Kent.*

——— *Voyage in the Vincennes*, 1829, '30.
Kent.

Dana, R. H., Jr. Two Years before the Mast (1).

This work from the forecastle has been listened to wherever ship sails and our language is spoken. It is truly a spirit-stirring voice.—*Bp. Potter.*

II. NORTHERN SEAS.

Forster's History of Northern Voyages and Discoveries, from 1497–1769.—*Kent.*

Coxe's Account of Russian Discoveries, between Asia and America.—*Kent.*

Phipp, Capt. Voyage to the Polar Regions, in 1773. Annexed to *Cook's First Voyage.*—*Kent.*

Leslie, Jameson, and Murray. Discoveries in the Polar Seas and Regions (1).—*Kent.*

Tytler's Discoveries on the Northern Coasts of America.
Kent.

Ross's Voyage to Baffin's Bay, in 1818.
Kent.

Parry's First Voyage to Baffin's Bay and Winter Harbor, 1819, '20.—*Kent.*

——— *Second Voyage to Hudson's Bay*, 1821, '22, '23. *Kent.*

——— *Third Voyage to Prince Regent's Inlet*, 1824–25. *Kent.*

Ross's Second Voyage in search of a North-West Passage, 1829–33.

For intrepidity, skill, perseverance, and suffering, these voyages of Ross and Parry are unparalleled. Nor did the severities of an arctic winter ever appear in more unmitigated horror. Nor were the utmost efforts of human contrivance ever more uselessly expended.—*Kent.*

Franklin, Sir John. First Journey to the Polar Sea, 1810–22.—*Kent.*

——— *Second Journey to the Polar Sea*, 1825–27. *Kent.*

Back, Capt. Journey to the same, in 1833–35.

These very authentic travels, like the voyages of Parry and Ross, have excited the curiosity and sympathies of the civilized world. They are indeed wonderful exhibitions of courage, skill, resolution, and manly virtue; and yet the frozen regions and seas into which they penetrated, are fit only for the receptacle of bears and seals, and bear frightful marks of the sterility and desolation of eternal winter.—*Kent.*

Scoresby, Wm. The Franklin Expedition and its Relief (1).

Richardson, Sir John. Arctic Searching Exploring Expedition (1).

A journal of a boat voyage through Rupert's Land and the Arctic Sea in search of Sir John Franklin.

Osborn, Lt. Arctic Journal—in Search of Sir John Franklin, 1851–2 (1).

VI.

BELLES LETTRES—ANCIENT.

I. GREEK ORATORY, PHILOSOPHY, AND POETRY.

Demosthenes, The Orations of (1).

Translated by LELAND.

The orations are distinguished for simplicity, ardor, and force; and they are translated with great ability and accuracy. Hume says the orations present to us models, which of all human compositions, approach the nearest to perfection. This eulogy appears to be extravagant, when we consider how rarely his orations are read and studied even by scholars and statesmen, or when we recur to the speeches of Pitt, Fox, Burke, Hamilton, or Ames, Webster, or Clay, or Brougham.—*Kent.*

Aristotle's Ethics and Politics (2).

Translated by Dr. GILLIES, the dignified historian of Greece.

The former were intended to explain and enforce the cardinal virtues of prudence, temperance, justice, and fortitude. It was the earliest effort of antiquity to establish a system of moral philosophy. His politics displayed his profound sagacity, and it is admitted that Cicero, Machiavel, Montesquieu, Bacon, and other statesmen, were largely indebted to Aristotle for the most solid of their speculations.—*Kent.*

——— *Ethics* (1).

By BROWNE. (*Bohn's Class. Lib.*)

Homer's Iliad and Odyssey (2).

Translated by POPE.

The former is also translated by Cowper (1) into English blank verse, with great accuracy and fidelity. It is the only translation which gives a true portrait of Homer. Pope's version is periphrastic and free to an amazing degree; but it will charm as long as the English language lasts, by reason of the matchless melody of its versification.—*Kent.*

Homer's Iliad (2).

Translated by W. MUMFORD.

This version of the Iliad in blank verse, by an American, is worthy o. study, both for its origin, and its excellence. It renders with great fidelity and felicity, in what Milton calls "our English heroic verse without rhyme," the simplicity, the sublimity, and all but the admirable modulation of the Homeric verse.—*Ch. King.*

Homer (1).

A literal Prose Translation. (*Bohn's Class. Lib.*)

Pope, for the beauty and perfection of versification, Mumford, for faithful and withal poetical version, and this prose translation, for an accurate comprehension of the noblest of poems, should each have his turn.—*Ch. King.*

Æschylus, The Tragedies of (2).

Translated by POTTER.

Nothing in all antiquity surpasses the bold and fiery genius, and pathos, of this father of Greek tragedy.—*Kent.*

——— Prose Translation (1). (*Bohn's Class. Lib.*)

——— *The Agamemnon.*

Translated into English Verse by JOHN CONINGTON.

An elegant translation, rendered extremely valuable by its numerous critical and explanatory notes.

Sophocles, The Tragedies of (1).

Translated by FRANKLIN, and again by DALE.—*Kent.*

Euripides (2).

Translated by R. POTTER.

——— Prose Translation (1). (*Bohn's Class. Lib.*)

Eminently grave, pathetic, and sublime productions.—*Kent.*

——— *Iphigenia in Tauris.*

Translated by Prof. GEO. J. ADLER.

An excellent translation by a promising man and ripe scholar.

Aristophanes (2).

Translated by WHEELWRIGHT.—*Kent.*

Plato (1).

By CARY, DAVIS, and BURGES. (*Bohn's Class. Lib.*)

The storehouse of ideas, of philosophy, of high morals, worthy to be read and meditated first after the Bible.—*Ch. King.*

Greek Anthology, Selections from (2).

By BLAND and MERIVALE.—*Ch. King.*

Mure, Col. History of Greek Literature (1).

The result of thorough study, of earnest admiration of Greek literature, and of acute personal investigation, especially as to the Odyssey, in tracing out on the spot the wanderings of Ulysses, and deducing from the which the conclusion that Homer's poems are his, and not a cento of fugitive ballads.—*Ch. King.*

Browne's History of Greek Classical Literature (1).

II. ROMAN ORATORY, PHILOSOPHY, AND POETRY.

Cicero's Works (1),

So far as they are translated.

His writings are transcendent. I recommend his Offices; his Tusculan Disputations; his Treatise on the Nature of the Gods; his Treatises on Old Age and Friendship; his Epistles, and his numerous and elaborate Orations. We need not look into Roman history beyond Cicero, for specimens of the perfection of Roman oratory, philosophy, and wisdom. The eventful life of Cicero; his splendid public services; his exalted patriotism; his surprising industry; his immense erudition; his profound sagacity; his incorruptible integrity; his almost Christian philosophy, are thoroughly apparent in his works, and elegantly delineated in Middleton's life of him.—*Kent.*

Pliny the Younger, The Epistles of (1).

Translated by MELMOTH.

They are exceedingly amusing and instructive portraits of Roman society and contemporary characters. He details the first irruption of Vesuvius, where his uncle perished.—*Kent.*

Lucan's Pharsalia (2).

Translated by Rowe into English verse.

It is an historical poem of the epic character, and displays the successful ambition of Julius Cæsar, and the inflexible perseverance of Cato.—*Kent.*

Terence, The Comedies of (1).

Translated by Colman.

Excellent.

Virgil, The Georgics of.

Translated by Sotheby.

——— *The Æneid of.*

Translated by Dryden.

These translations are much admired for elegance and harmony. That of Dryden is much disfigured, to my taste, by his triplets. The poems themselves are enchanting. Sir Walter Scott says, that Dryden has completely surpassed all that have preceded or succeeded him, in communicating Virgil's ideas, with force and energy equal to his own. His version of the sixth Æneid is beautiful and unequalled.—*Kent.*

——— Prose translation. (1) (*Bohn's Class. Lib.*)

Horace. Odes, Satires, and Epistles.

Translated by Dr. Francis,

In faithful and beautiful verse. Rather than not to be acquainted with the subjects, and some of the beauties of Virgil and Horace, I would read them in the prose translations of Davidson and Smart. They are true and elegant prose translations, and no person can understand the Roman manners and Roman mind under Augustus accurately, without being well versed in Horace. —*Kent.*

——— Prose translation (1). (*Bohn's Class. Lib.*)

Juvenal's Satires.

Translated by Gifford.

The translation in English verse is masterly, and unites fidelity with spirit. It is the best poetical version of a classic in the English language. Many of Juvenal's descriptions are gross and offensive, but they do not corrupt. Their tendency is to excite disgust and horror, and the vices of the age are chastised by Juvenal, with a tragic tone and awe-inspiring indignation.—*Kent.*

Persius, Aulus Flaccus. Satires (2).
Translated by Rev. F. Howes.

Martial, M. Valerius. Select Epigrams (2).
Translated by Hay.

The most of his epigrams are acute and appropriate. Their multitude and proportionate excellence render the almost inexhaustible and always lively wit of this poet admirable.—*Eschenburgh.*

Catullus, Caius Valerius. Poems (2).
Translated by Hon. G. Lamb.

The friend of Cicero and Cornelius Nepos. He was the first of the Romans who imitated successfully the Greek lyric poetry.—*Bp. Potter.*

Seneca, Lucius Annæus (2).

His tragedies are in general removed from the noble simplicity of Greek tragedy, and are mostly of very defective plot and execution, though not without single poetic beauties.—*Eschenburgh.*

Ovid's Metamorphoses.

Translated by Dryden, Pope, and others.

——— Prose translation (2). (*Bohn's Class. Lib.*)

Bohn's Classical Series and *Harpers' Classical Library* contain among the best translations of the ancient classics.

The following works ought to be read or examined in connection with the Roman writers:—

Dunlop's History of Roman Literature (2).
Kent.

Browne's History of Roman Literature (1).

Crusius's Lives of the Roman Poets (2).
Kent.

Adams's Roman Antiquities (2).
Kent.

Smith's Dictionary of Greek and Roman Antiquities (1).

VII.

BELLES LETTRES—MODERN.

I. GENERAL LITERATURE AND PHILOSOPHY OF EUROPE.

Hallam's View of Europe, during the Middle Ages (1).

A work of profound research, and displaying a free and vigorous spirit of inquiry and criticism.—*Kent.*

——— *Introduction to the Literature of Europe, during the* 15*th,* 16*th, and* 17*th Centuries* (1).

This is a production of the greatest value, and distinguished like his other work, for research, judgment, taste, and elegance.—*Kent.*

Staël, Madame de. Germany (2).

This work has been extolled to the skies. It is a sweeping view of society, manners, institutions, and literature, in every part of the immense and complicated empire of Germany; and it well displays her exalted genius, her intense feelings, her extensive knowledge, and profound reflections.—*Kent.*

Guizot's History of Civilization in Europe (1).

This is a very interesting work, and contains the evidences of deep meditation, noble principles, and enlarged philosophy. The author is a conservative, a statesman, and a Christian.—*Kent.*

Burke's Reflections, and other Writings, on the French Revolution, and on European Policy (1).

All of Burke's works ought to be read and studied. They prove his wonderful genius, his taste, his sagacity, his goodness, his wisdom, his judgment, his varied virtues, and his eloquence.—*Kent.*

Sismondi's Historical View of the Literature of the South of Europe (1). Translated by Roscoe.

This celebrated, voluminous, and eloquent writer, maintains a distinguished reputation.—*Kent.*

Shaw's Outlines of English Literature (1).

Foster's Handbook of Modern European Literature (2).

Smyth, Wm. Historical Fancies (2).

Nichols, J. Literary Anecdotes of the Eighteenth Century (2).

Menzel's History of German Literature (1).

A valuable history of the literature of Germany, which should command the earnest attention of the student.

Ticknor's History of Spanish Literature (1).

Without aspiring to the suggestive originality of Bouterwek, or to the terse and powerful analysis of Hallam, Mr. Ticknor has produced a record which may be read with general satisfaction, and will be lastingly valued for reference.—*Edin. Rev.*

Talvi (Mrs. Dr. Robinson). Historical View of the Language and Literature of the Sclavic Nations (1).

Vericour's Course of French Literature (2).
Edited by W. S. Chase.

Admirable for the valuable notes contributed by its editor.

Beloe's Anecdotes of Literature and Scarce Books (2).

Light and agreeable reading.

Montesquieu's Spirit of Laws (1),

Is a work of general interest and application on government and public policy, with the exception of his discussion of the feudal laws, which may belong to jurisprudence. No work excited more attention or a greater spirit of inquiry in the middle of the last century. And though it abounds in fanciful theories and obsolete matter, it is still worthy of the study of statesmen and scholars, as well as of the legal antiquarian.—*Kent.*

Pascal's Provincial Letters (1),

Are distinguished for wit, taste, bitter irony, and acute criticism. Gibbon said that he perused Pascal's Provincial Letters every year with new pleasure. D'Aguesseau goes further, and doubts whether the Philippics of Demosthenes, or Cicero, offer any thing more forcible or more perfect. They were translated into English in 1816.—*Kent.*

Guizot's Democracy in France (2).

Longfellow's Poets and Poetry of Europe (1).

Hedge's Prose Writers of Germany (2).

Schlegel, A. W. History of Dramatic Literature (2).
From the German.

Schlegel, Frederick. Philosophy of History (1).
From the German.

——— *Lectures on Modern History* (1).

The influence which the brothers Schlegel have exerted on belles-lettres in general, especially in promoting a more correct understanding of the literature of the Middle Ages, is very great, and extends far beyond their native country. They will be remembered in the history of literature as two minds of uncommon vigor.—*Enc. Amer.*

Miller's Philosophy of History (1).

II. ESSAYS, CRITICISM, LITERARY HISTORY.

Hallam's Introduction to the Literature of Europe (1).

A work of great industry and acuteness. It displays a knowledge, extensive, various, and profound, and a mind equally distinguished by the amplitude of its grasp and by the delicacy of its tact.—*Edin. Rev.*

Bacon's Essays and Advancement of Learning (1).

No English writer surpassed Bacon, in the fervor and brilliancy of style, in force of expression, or in richness and significance of imagery. He has treated philosophy with all the splendor, yet with none of the vagueness of poetry, and sometimes his style possesses a degree of conciseness very rarely to be found in the compositions of the Elizabethan age.—*Chambers.*

La Rochefoucauld's Maxims (2).

Among the books in ancient and modern times which record the conclusions of observing men on the moral qualities of their fellows, a high place should be reserved for "The Maxims of Rochefoucauld."—*Hallam.*

Selden, John. Table Talk (1).

It is full of vigor, raciness, and a kind of scorn of the half-learned. His style is often labored and uncouth, although his speeches and conversations are humorous and clear.—*Hallam.*

Walton and Cotton's Angler (1).

This has long been a standard work in our language, and it will ever remain a favorite for its quiet philosophising spirit and quaintness. It is a book after one's own heart.

Chesterfield, Lord. Letters to his Son (3).

Amid much of loose morality there is in these volumes, especially for the young man whose judgment is somewhat matured, much that may profit in the formation of manners, which are the minor morals, and upon which, as they are rude or polished, deferential or presuming, success in life may depend, at least as much as upon more substantial qualities. In our state of society much in these letters is inapplicable altogether; but human nature is the same under every form of government or phase of society. The advice of Lord Chesterfield to his son, when it bears upon the general interest and motives of our nature, and as it exemplifies the advantages of a polished exterior, and a winning personal bearing, may be usefully studied.—*Ch. King.*

The Spectator and Tattler (1).

These earliest of the regular essays were written by Steele and Addison, and their merits were transcendent in contributing to reform the taste, purify the pleasures, and elevate the morals and literature of the nation. Addison's papers in the Spectator were designated by one of the letters of the muse Clio, and they are distinguished not less for purity of taste and solidity of judgment, than for the chaste and graceful simplicity of their style.—*Kent.*

The Rambler and Idler (1).

Most of the papers in these two works were written by Dr. Johnson, and are characterized by great force of expression and depth of thought.—*Bp. Potter.*

The Guardian, The Adventurer, Observer and Mirror (2).

The first of these "British Classics" is adorned with papers from Pope and Berkeley, as well as from Steele; the second, intended as a sequel to the Rambler, is from the pen of Hawkesworth and Dr. Johnson; the papers in the Observer were all written by Cumberland, and those in the Mirror principally by Mackenzie, author of the "Man of Feeling."—*Bp. Potter.*

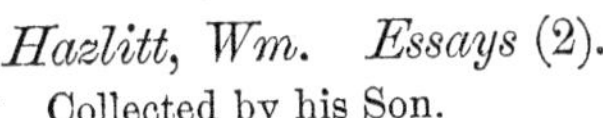

Hazlitt, Wm. *Essays* (2).

Collected by his Son.

——— *The Winterslow Essays and Characters* (2).

These essays on subjects of taste and literature are deservedly popular. He is a writer of force and ingenuity, of illustration, strength, terseness, and vivacity.—*Penny Cyclo.*

——— *Spirit of the Age* (2).

——— *Characters of Shakespeare.*

There is scarcely to be found in the whole circle of English literature a finer specimen of accumulative eloquence than the account of the intellectual life of Coleridge in the Spirit of the Age.—*Penny Cyc.*

Hall, Robert. *Works* (2).

A repository of noble thoughts and admirable style, and on religious topics of great theological learning.—*Ch. King.*

Montagu, Basil. *Selections from the Works of Taylor, Hooker, Barrow, South, Latimer, Brown, Milton, and Bacon* (1).

Excellent selections from some of the most distinguished of the "Old English Divines."

Leighton, Archbishop. *Works* (1).

To be read with profit for the life and conduct of the eminent prelate in stirring times, not less than for its eloquent theological disquisitions.—*Ch. King.*

Littleton, Lord. *Letters* (2).

A supposititious work, but remarkable for its pure flowing idiomatic English.—*Ch. King.*

Rejected Addresses (2).

Much of the interest attached to these celebrated addresses being local and transient, is lost, but they will always deserve attention.—*Ch. King.*

Jameson, Mrs. *Female Characters of Shakespeare* (2).

I have endeavored to illustrate the various modifications of which the female character is susceptible, with their causes and results. I have illustrated certain positions by examples, and leave my readers to deduce the moral themselves, and draw their own inferences.—*Preface.*

Southey, Robert. Essays (1).

——— *The Doctor* (1).

The latter of these works is full of strange knowledge, and unexpected turns of thought and argument, and cannot fail to command interest.—*Ch. King.*

D'Israeli's Amenities of Literature (1).

Though at first sight the work appears to be a series of essays, yet it will be found on examination, that the subject of each essay is a salient point of our vernacular literature.—*London Athen.*

Lamb, Charles. Works (1).

His delicious "Essays" are full of wisdom, pregnant with genuine wit, abound in true pathos, and have a rich vein of humor running through them all.—*Hall.*

Coleridge, Samuel Taylor. Table Talk (1).

The object of this work is to show the conversations of Mr. Coleridge, and its contents may be taken as pretty strong presumptive evidence that his ordinary manner was plain and direct, and even when, as sometimes happened, he seemed to ramble from the road, and to lose himself in a wilderness of digressions, he was at that very time working out his foreknown conclusion through an almost miraculous logic.—*Preface.*

——— *The Friend* (2).

This work is a friend indeed, venerable, yet familiar, thoughtful, and of the kindest, noblest feelings, teaching wisdom for meditation, and alluring to meditation by presenting to the mind, not amusement only, but

"Flowers
Of sober tints, and herbs of medicinal powers."—*No. Am. Rev.*

——— *Biographia Literaria* (2).

De Quincy, Thos. Confessions of an Opium Eater (1).

——— *The Cæsars* (1). *Biographical Essays, &c.* (1).

Macaulay's Miscellanies (2).

Brilliant, and always instructive, evidencing thorough study and much thought, though not always accurate in their decisions.

Jeffreys, Francis. Essays (2).

Stephen, Sir James. Essays (2).

Originally contributed to the Edinburgh Review.

Wilson, Prof. John (Christopher North). Recreations (1).

Most, if not all of these papers, originally appeared in Blackwood. They are of various degrees of merit, though many of them breathe a genial humor and pathos rarely excelled.

Carlyle's Sartor Resartus (2).

——— *Heroes and Hero Worship* (3).

Pictures vividly painted, though not always true to nature.—*Ch. King.*

Everett, Edward. Essays and Speeches (1).

Judicious, eloquent, instructive.—*Bp. Potter.*

Webster's Speeches and Writings (1).

A model of English and manly eloquence.—*Ch. King.*

Verplanck, G. C. Essays (1).

His style is pure, perspicuous, and beautifully elaborate; not always perhaps sufficiently spirited and flowing, and sometimes cumbersome and heavy. —*N. Y. Rev.*

Emerson, Ralph Waldo. Essays (2).

——— *Representative Men* (2).

A remarkable series of eloquent essays, suggestive always, if not always sound.—*Ch. King.*

Channing's Essays and Discourses (2).

Few among the present or recent philosophical writers in our own language, says the *North American Review*, have exhibited the same originality, depth, and power of thought, so happily combined with the vigor and beauty of language, which are necessary to give them effect.

Landor, Walter Savage. Works (1).

His imaginary conversations, entertaining and characteristic. His poems, Sheba and Count Julien, although excessively admired and praised by Southey, are now little read or talked of.—*Ch. King.*

Drake. Literary Hours (2).

Irving's Essays, under the title of Geoffrey Crayon (1).

His remarkable elegance, sustained sweetness, and distinct and delicate painting, place him in the very front rank of the masters of our language.—*Griswold.*

Hunt, Leigh. Indicator and Companion, and other Essays (2).

Hunt, as a writer and critic, is seldom very profound, perhaps, but always sparkling with a singular effervescence of animal spirits, and we are not sure that his easy, pleasant, good-humored chat, has not done more than Hazlitt's graver tone, to disseminate a taste for rich and healthy literature.—*Shaw.*

Dana, Richard H. Prose Works (2).

An American author, who should be well studied by all lovers of fine and sterling English. He is worthy to be ranked among the first of living writers.

Bethune, Rev. Geo. W., D.D. Orations and Occasional Discourses (2).

Helps, Arthur. Friends in Council. Companions of my Solitude. Essays written in the Intervals of Business (1).

All excellent, philosophical, and breathing a most philanthropic spirit.

Mitchell, Donald G. (Ik Marvel). The Lorgnette (2).

Elegant, opinionated, and natural.—*Ch. King.*

Sumner, Charles. Orations (2).

Giles, Henry. Lectures and Essays (2).

Whipple, Edwin P. Essays and Reviews (2).

Lowell, J. R. Letters on the Old English Poets (2).

Laconics; or, the best Words of the best Authors (1).

A useful work of reference for aphorisms, and long referred to as the best of this class of publications.

Household Words (2).

Conducted by CHARLES DICKENS.

Schiller's Works (2).

Bohn's Standard Library, 4 *vols.*

III. POETRY.

English.

Poetry is musick in words, and musick is poetry in sound, both excellent sauce; but they have lived and died poor that made them their meat.—*Fuller.*

Warton's History of English Poetry (2).

This work is justly considered as a vast store-house of facts connected with early English literature. Its arrangement facilitates the reader in research, and enables him to see without transposition the gradual improvements in poetry and the progression in our language.—*Chambers.*

Chaucer. Works (2).

The father of English poetry. Those who prefer to read as he wrote, would do well to give The Knight's Tale, The Squire's Tale, The Clerke's Tale, and The Nun Priest's Tale, a careful perusal. These four form part of the "Canterbury Tales," and are considered as the best of that collection. The Flower and the Leaf is an exquisite poem, and was an especial favorite of the poet Campbell. The House of Fame, a fine allegory, is also well worthy of study. Chaucer has been modernized in part by Charles Cowden Clarke; and also by R. H. Horne and others; and by Ch. D. Deshler, to whom the student would do well to refer.

Spenser. The Faërie Queene (1).

The reputation of Spenser rests upon this poem, and, says the Edinburgh Encyclopædia, "with all its defects, it possesses many of the noblest of the poetic graces—sublimity, pathos, the most unrivalled fertility of conception, and exquisite vividness of description." We would commend the version by Mrs. Kirkland, in modern verse, to those who wish to enjoy this exquisite poem, freed from its impurities.

Drayton, Michael. Polyolbion (2).

A poem which, of its kind (topographical and legendary), probably has never been equalled in any other language, both in extent and elegance; nor can any one read a portion of it without admiration for its learned and highly gifted author.—*Bp. Potter.*

Drummond. Sonnets (2).

Polished and elegant, free from conceit and bad taste, in fine unblemished English.—*Hallam.*

Milton, John (1).

Of the sublimity of the genius of Milton, and the depth and variety of his learning, there can be no difference of opinion; and in respect to the first, his own countrymen will scarcely admit he has ever been equalled.—*Enc. Am.*

We would especially commend to the reader, "Paradise Lost," "L'Allegro," "Il Penseroso," and "Comus."

Dryden (1).

The best specimens are his "Fables," "Alexander's Feast," and "Absalom and Achipotel." Congreve says of the Poet:—"No man has written in any language so much, and so various matter, and in so various manner, well."

Butler. Hudibras (1).

The work of perhaps the greatest master of the comic or burlesque species of satiric writing, who ever lived,—a strange and singular genius, whose powers of ridicule were incomparable. In originality of conception and brilliancy of form, his work is unequalled. Indeed, "Hudibras" is one of those productions which may be said to stand alone in literature.—*Shaw.*

Parnell. The Hermit, and Night Piece on Death (2).

Addison. Hymns. Letter from Italy. The Campaign (2).

Pope. His Poetical Works generally (1).

His quick and critical judgment was masterly, and the harmony and melody of his verse unrivalled. The argument of the "Essay on Man" was written by Bolingbroke, and versified by Pope.

Thomson. The Seasons. Castle of Indolence (1).

His greatest poetical merit undoubtedly stands most conspicuous in the "Seasons." Its diction is somewhat cumbrous and labored, but energetic and expressive; but perhaps no poem has ever been more and more deservedly popular.—*Aikin.*

Collins. Odes and Pastorals, or Oriental Eclogues (2).

Nothing can surpass their exquisite pathos and beautiful simplicity.—*Kent.*

Young. *Night Thoughts on Life, Death, and Immortality; Paraphrase on Part of the Book of Job; Tragedy of Zanga* (1). —*Kent.*

Gray. *On a Prospect of Eton College: The Bard; The Progress of Poesy; Elegy in a Country Churchyard* (1).

The "Elegy in a Country Churchyard" must be a favorite, so long as the English language exists; and though not marked with any striking originality, yet it is illustrated with such exquisite taste, and so much grace, that it is a masterpiece of poetic handling.

Shenstone. *Schoolmistress. Pastoral Ballads, in Four Parts* (2).

The "Schoolmistress" is most delightfully quaint and ludicrous, yet so true to nature, that it has all the force and vividness of a painting of Teniers or Wilkie. The Ballads are esteemed the finest English poems of that order.

Akenside. *The Pleasures of the Imagination* (2).

Seldom read continuously through. Its finest passages, by frequent quotation, are well known.

Falconer. *Shipwreck* (2).

The truth of this poem is one of its greatest attractions. It has the rare merit of being a pleasing and interesting poem.

Goldsmith. *Traveller, Deserted Village, and Retaliation* (1).

His poetry natural, melodious, affecting, and beautifully descriptive, finds an echo in every bosom.—*Bp. Potter.*

Johnson. *London. Variety of Human Wishes* (1).

Scott always said, that he received more pleasure in reading these poems than any other poetical composition he could mention.

Beattie. *The Minstrel. The Hermit* (1).
King.

Cowper. *The Task* (1).

His pages are full of scenery, and pictures of life and manners, dignified by the highest sentiments, and made interesting by the most tender touches of the social affections.—*Ed. Enc.*

Burns (1).

Among many, may be mentioned the following Poems as excellent, viz.:—"The Vision;" "The Cotter's Saturday Night;" "Tam O'Shanter;" "The Twa Dogs;" "The Brigs of Ayr," &c. &c.

"The Cotter's Saturday night," is one of the truest and most tender living pictures of rustic life that has ever been traced by the hand of the poet.

Campbell. Pleasures of Hope. Gertrude of Wyoming (1).

The poetry of Campbell is universally felt, and therefore universally appreciated.—*Mrs. Hall.*

Rogers. Pleasures of Memory. Italy (1).

His poems are not remarkable for passion or vigor, but they are surpassingly sweet, touching, and correct.—*Mrs. Hall.*

Crabbe. The Borough. Nancy Dawson (1).

The latter of these poems was read to Fox on his death-bed.

Southey (1).

The best of his poems are Thalaba and Roderick.—*Kent.*

Scott. Lay of the Last Minstrel. Marmion. Lady of the Lake (1).—*Kent.*

Wordsworth. Excursion. Lyrical Ballads and Laodamia (1).

He is ever true to nature. Passages from his works have become as familiar as household words, and are perpetually called into use to give strong and apt expressions to the thoughts and feelings of others. His poems are full of beauties, of original thoughts, of fine sympathies, and grave yet cheerful wisdom.—*Mrs. Hall.*

Byron. Prisoner of Chillon. The Giaour. The Bride of Abydos. The Corsair. Childe Harold's Pilgrimage (2).—*Kent.*

Shelley. Prometheus Unbound. Alastor. The Cenci (2).

Keats. Hyperion. Ode to Pan. Eve of St. Agnes (2).

A Poet, whose untimely death was much to be lamented.

Henry Kirke White. Poems (2).

Another youthful Poet, early snatched from us by the hand of death. He gave promise of great genius.

Coleridge. Poems, particularly Christabel, the Ancient Mariner, and Genevieve. (1).

Some of the most perfect examples that our language can supply, are to be found among his poems; full of the simplest and purest nature, yet pregnant with the deepest and most subtile philosophy.—*Aikin.*

Pollok. Course of Time (3).

Thos. Hood. Poems (1).

More tender, more graceful, or more beautifully wrought lyrics, are scarcely to be found in our language.—*Bp. Potter.*

Mrs. Hemans. Poems (2).

Elegant and pure in thought and language, sometimes sublime and religious.

Tennyson. Poems generally (1).

His poems are so thickly studded with evidences of manly force and exquisite tenderness, with feelings so true and fancies so felicitous, clothed in a music often peculiar in its flow, but never cloying, as to substantiate Mr. Tennyson's claim to a high rank among modern poets.—*London Athenæum.*

Bulwer. King Arthur (2).

A poem which deserves a high rank; full of beauties, and written in a forcible and elevated style.

Elliott. Corn Law Rhymes (2).

Ch. King.

Montgomery, James. Poems (1).

Baillie, Joanna. Tragedies (2).

AMERICAN.

Griswold, R. W. Poets and Poetry of America (1).

——— ——— *Female Poets of America* (1).

Excellent Encyclopædias of the minor poets of our country. They exhibit much good taste, judgment, and fairness in their arrangement.

5

Allston, Washington. Sylphs of the Seasons. The Two Painters, and the Paint King (3).

Allston is one of the oldest of the "Poets of America;" and the three pieces selected give an excellent specimen of his style.

Dana, Richard H. The Buccaneer (2).

Is his largest, and perhaps best poem. He is a disciple of the school of Coleridge, Wordsworth, &c., now familiarly known as the "Lake School."

Sprague, Charles. Poems (2).

Bryant, W. C. Poems (1).

No poet has described with more fidelity the beauties of the Creation, nor sung in nobler lays the praises of the Creator. He is a translator of the silent language of the Universe to the World.—*Griswold.*

Drake, Joseph R. The Culprit Fay (1).
Ch. King.

Brainerd, John G. Poems (2).
Ch. King.

Halleck, Fitz Greene. Poems (1).

Whether serious or satirical, his pieces are admirable. There are few finer martial Lyrics than his Marco Bozarris.—*Bp. Potter.*

Longfellow. Poems (1).

Elaborate and touching, his Evangeline is the most perfect specimen perhaps extant of the rhythm and melody of the English Hexameter.—*Ch. King.*

Holmes, Oliver Wendell. Poems (1).

A poet, in whose writings sparkle, like gems, the outpourings of a brilliant wit and graceful fancy.

Lowell, James Russell. Poems (1).

Emerson, Ralph Waldo. Poems (1).

Full of deep thought, and fine writing.

Mrs. Sigourney's Poems (3).

Davidson (L. and M. M.). Poems (3).

Mrs. Welby's Poems (3).

Willis, N. P. Poems (2), *particularly his Sacred Poems.*

Whittier, J. G. Poems (2).

EUROPEAN.

Dante. Inferno (1).

Translated by H. F. CARY.

Dante's works are important chiefly in three respects: as the production of one of the greatest men that ever lived, as one of the keys of the history of his times, and as exhibiting the state of learning, theology, and politics, in that age.—*Enc. Am.*

Ariosto. Orlando Furioso (3).

Translated by ROSE.

This romance is a complete wilderness, in which there is no continued path, but in which are to be seen at every step the most magnificent scenes, the most picturesque prospects, the richest fruits, and the most brilliant flowers. Ariosto excels, in narrative and description, and is distinguished by a nervous, expressive, and unaffected style.—*Nor. Amer. Rev.*

The translator has rendered justice to the humor and beauty of his author.

Jerusalem Delivered (1).

Translated by FAIRFAX, Edited by LEIGH HUNT.

This elegant poem abounds with all the pleasing description of tender scenes, the animated representation of battles, and the majestic flow of language, which so much captivate and overpower the reader in the pages of Homer and Virgil.—*Blake.*

The edition by Mr. Hunt ranks far above the greater number of those who have aspired to make the readers of our language familiar with the poetry of other lands.

La Fontaine. Fables (2).

Translated by ELIZUR WRIGHT.

A most excellent translation of a work which belongs to a class that will ever remain popular.

Brooks, C. T. Translation. Lays and Ballads from Uhland, Korner, and others (2).

Carlyle. *Specimens of Arabian Poetry* (3).

Bowring. *Specimens of Russian Poets* (3).

——— *Poetry of the Magyars* (3).

Costello, Miss. *The Rose Garden of Persia* (3).
Translated from Persian.

Somers. *Selections from Modern French Poets* (3).

Schiller. *The Poems and Ballads of* (2).
Translated by BULWER.

Bowring. *Poetry of Spain* (2).

Wieland. *Oberon* (3).
Translated by SOTHEBY.

These works will enable the reader to form a very good idea of the poetry of some of the European and Asiatic states, the selections having been made by persons of undoubted ability and taste.

IV. DRAMA.

It is the wisdom of government to permit plays, as it is the prudence of a carter to put bells upon his horses, to make them carry their burden cheerfully.—SIR W. D'AVENANT.

Shakespeare's Dramatic Works (1),

No one should ever cease reading. Begin with the Tragedies; for it has been finely said by Hazlitt, "That the great difference between the productions of the great bard and all others, is their wonderful truth and individuality of conception. The poet may be said to identify himself with the character he wishes to represent, and his characters become real beings of flesh and blood, and speak like men, and not like authors. His plays alone are properly expressions of the passions, and not descriptions of them." Dr. Johnson thought Shakespeare's Comedies better than his Tragedies, and gives in his supreme egotism, as a reason, that *he* was more at home in the one than in the other. And yet, while there are many writers who have been considered by some of our best and most learned critics, as being equal to the bard in Comedy, never has there been known in the world a Tragedy that would make even a tolerable approach to "Hamlet," "Lear," or "Othello." Truly there is no book next to the Bible, more fit to be the daily companion of men, than Shakespeare; for as it is beautifully expressed by Shaw, "his wit is unbounded, his passion inimitable, and his splendor unequalled; and over these varied glories he has thrown a halo of human sympathy no less tender than his genius was immeasurable and profound; a light reflected from the most gentle, generous, loving spirit, that ever glowed within a human heart—the consummate union of the Beautiful and Good."

Lamb's Specimens of English Dramatic Poets, who lived about the Time of Shakespeare (1).

A careful and judicious collation of the beauties of Jonson, Massinger, Ford, Otway, Lee, Beaumont, Fletcher, and others of the contemporaries of Shakespeare, by a genial and master hand.

For those who would prefer to read whole plays of these authors, we would recommend the "Every Man in his Humor," and "Alchemist," of Jonson, the "Philaster," and the "Elder Brother," of Beaumont and Fletcher, the "New Way to Pay Old Debts," of Massinger, and the "Broken Heart," of Ford, as giving the best specimens of the writings of the most worthy of the brilliant galaxy of Dramatists, who shed such lustre around the "Age of Elizabeth."

Among our more modern writers, it will be necessary only to name a few, that have received the decided mark of public favor. The Cato of Addison; Sheridan's School for Scandal, and The Rivals; Goldsmith's She Stoops to Conquer; Colman's Jealous Wife: Macklin's Man of the World. And to come down to more recent authors, Talfourd's Ion; The Virginius, and Wife of Knowles; Tobin's Honey Moon; Taylor's Philip of Van Artevelde, and The Virgin Widow; and the Tragedies of Joanna Baillie, will give the reader as comprehensive a view of the modern stage, in all its varieties, as it is necessary to obtain, though there is no more attractive or instructive reading than a good play.

The "Faust" of Goethe (2),

Translated by HAYWARD, and

Schiller's "Robbers," Translated (1),

Are commended to the attention of the reader. The first bears the mark of the great genius of its author. Hayward's translation is by far the most satisfactory and pleasing.

Of American Dramatic writers, we can but mention the name of Boker, who, in his Calaynos, and other works, gives promise of greater and more lasting fame, which we trust yet to see fulfilled.

V. FINE ARTS.

"What has pleased, and continues to please, is likely to please again; hence are derived the rules of art; and on this immovable foundation, they must for ever stand."—SIR J. REYNOLDS.

Lanzi. *History of Painting in Italy* (1).

Cleghorn. *Ancient and Modern Art* (2).

Goethe. *Essays on Art* (1).
From the German, by WARD.

Taylor. *History of Fine Arts in Great Britain* (2).

Jameson, Mrs. *Sacred and Legendary Art* (2).

——— ——— *Legends of the Monastic Orders* (2).

Hazlitt, Wm. *Essays on Art* (1).

Allston. *Lectures on Art* (1).

Ruskin. *Modern Painters* (1).

——— *Seven Lamps of Architecture* (1).

——— *Stones of Venice* (1).

Flaxman. *Lectures on Scripture* (2).

——— *Illustrations of the Iliad, Odyssey, &c.* (2).

Retzsch. *Outlines of Faust* (2).

Winckleman, John. *History of Ancient Art* (1).

Burney. *History of Music* (1).

Hogarth. *Memoirs of the Musical Drama* (1).

Dunlap's History of the Rise and Progress of the Arts of Design in the United States (2).

With much prejudice, there is much industry in these volumes, and information not elsewhere readily to be found.——*Ch. King.*

VI. PROSE FICTION.

"I had often thought that a Story-teller is born as well as a Poet."—STEELE.

Dunlop. History of Fiction (2).

Kent.

Cervantes. Don Quixote (1).

It is to this work that Cervantes owes his transcendent fame; and Hallam says of it: "There are few books of moral philosophy which display as deep an insight into the mechanism of the mind as Don Quixote. And when we look at the fertility of invention, the general probability of the events, and the great simplicity of the story, wherein no artifices are practised to create suspense, or complicate the action, we shall think Cervantes fully deserving of the glory that attends this monument of his genius."

Le Sage. Gil Blas (1).

A work that has procured for itself a place upon the pinnacle of literature. It is the most successful work of fiction that has ever emanated from a Frenchman.

Fenelon. Telemachus (1).

The beauties of this work are very numerous. The descriptions, and indeed the whole tone of the book, have a charm of grace, something like the pictures of Guido.—*Hallam.*

Richardson, Samuel. Clarissa Harlowe. Sir Charles Grandison (2).

The former has been regarded as his master-piece; and Rousseau was of opinion that there was no romance in any language to be compared to it. Richardson was distinguished for the purity of his morals, his deep knowledge of the human heart, his minute and thorough delineation of character, and his powers of pathetic description. The thread of his story is excessively prolix, and his narration is so slow as to vex the reader, and his characters too stiff and formal to suit the taste and manners of the age, and these novels are accordingly laid on the upper shelf. But Clarissa is an admirable novel, and the madness of Clementina in Sir Charles is full of exquisite strokes of nature and passion. Dr. Wharton says it is equal to the madness of Lear.—*Kent.*

Fielding and Smollett's Novels (1).

They contain the most just and lively delineations of society and manners in common and familiar life, during the reigns of George I. and II. They abound in striking incident, brilliant wit and humor, and bold and graphic paintings of character. Fielding is supposed to have been next to Shakespeare in wit and knowledge of mankind; and his Tom Jones has the genius and contrivance of an epic poem. But these celebrated romance writers partook of the gross and licentious taste too prevalent in that age; and we recur with satisfaction to subsequent novelists, who "bear no tokens of those sable streams."—*Kent.*

Sterne. Tristam Shandy (1).

The charm of this work consists in the easy, rambling style, in the exquisite touches of pathos and humor that alternately glow and sparkle in its pages, in the familiarity established between the reader and the fantastic, gossiping author, and above all in the masterly delineations of its many admirably conceived characters.—*Shaw.*

De Foe. Robinson Crusoe (1).

One of the most charming original fictions the world has ever seen, and which will be treasured so long as the English language exists.

Walpole, Horace. Castle of Otranto (2).

Written with elegance, and not eclipsed in interest by any modern romance.—*Ch. King.*

Johnson. Rasselas (1).

A work which has long been regarded as a classic among works of fiction.

Goldsmith. Vicar of Wakefield (1).

A work which has been read, translated, and admired by the whole civilized world. Its charming simplicity of style, true pathos, and gentle humor, commend it to the heart of every one; and his must be a stubborn nature, that can read unmoved the story of the trials and joys of the "Poor Vicar."

Mackenzie, Henry. Man of Feeling (2).

An imitator of Sterne, with more taste and delicacy, but inferior to him in originality and humor.

Moore, Dr. John. Zeluco and Mordaunt (2).

Ch. King.

Mrs. Radcliff's Mysteries of Udolpho, and The Italian (3).

Ch. King.

Crabbe's Tales (1).

Ch. King.

Godwin's Caleb Williams (2).

Ch. King.

Goethe. Wilhelm Meister (1).

Translated by CARLYLE.

The best of the fictions of Goethe—which have ever been considered as ranking at the head of this branch of German literature.

Richter, Jean Paul. Flowers. Fruit and Thorn Pieces (2).

A charming fiction, full of deep and earnest thought, studded with bright, sparkling fancy.

Edgeworth, Maria. Novels and Tales (1).

These may be safely recommended for constant perusal. They are full of excellent moral teachings, and good sense.

Austen, Jane. The Novels of (1).

Contain admirable delineations of the interior life of the rural gentry of England.

Scott, Sir Walter. Novels and Romances (1).

Every volume—every page is to be read. What novel, or what dialogue is there in Scott, over which the reader may not pause and admire?—*Kent.*

Bulwer. Rienzi. Last Days of Pompeii (2).

He is celebrated for his genius, enthusiasm, and power of description; but he is deficient in practical good sense, and simple delineation of the characters and sympathies that belong to actual life.—*Kent.*

Among his later productions, "The Caxton's," "Harold," and "My Novel," deserve a higher rank than has generally been accorded to the works of this author.

Warren, Dr. Samuel. Ten Thousand a Year (1).

A work of undeniable skill and genius, and which gives a vivid and impressive picture of modern English society.

James's Novels, particularly his historical tales (2).
Kent.

Dickens, Charles. Novels and Tales (1 *and* 2).

Dickens is an author of whom England may well be proud; for his works ennoble humanity, and appeal with a sure sympathy to all that is good in our common nature. The series of Christmas tales are especially commended for the benevolent, genial spirit which they express; and, says Shaw, "they display a degree of fancy and grace which is every way worthy of the object for which they were written—the noble aim of inspiring the rich and happy with sympathy and compassion for the poor." They breathe the very spirit of Christmas time—kindly, genial charity, and the truest sympathy for the friendless and suffering of mankind. His name will go down to posterity as a philanthropist and benefactor to the human race.

Thackeray, W. M. Vanity Fair, and Pendennis (1).

His works are full of fine and powerful writing, of wit, and a rare fancy.

Bronte, Charlotte. Jane Eyre, and Shirley (2).

Two of the most remarkable novels of the present day, and the more so, from being the production of a writer whose previous view in life had been limited to a very narrow circle. They possess great originality and true genius—a rare merit in works of fiction of the present day.

Santine, Mdme. di. Picciola (1).
From the French.

A beautiful little romance, which appeals most earnestly to the kindlier feelings and sympathies.

Manzini. I Promessi Sposi (2).
From the Italian.

A work of talent, and worthy of perusal.

Willoughby, Lady. Diary, and its Sequel (2).

A charming fiction, with all the truth of reality.—*Ch. King.*

Bremer, Frederika. Novels (2).

Especially "Home," and "The Neighbors." Charming pictures of domestic life, cleverly written, and inculcating a love of home and home enjoyments. The most of the series of the novels of this author have been well translated by Mary Howitt.

Kingsley, Rev. E. M. Alton Locke. Yeast (2).

Works of powerful interest, descriptive of the sufferings of the lower classes in England. Written by a sympathizer.—*Ch. King.*

Mrs. Sherwood's Stories and Tales,

Will all, or nearly all, prove profitable reading.

Miss Burney's Evelina (1).

Miss Sewell's Stories,

Devoted to the interests of the Episcopal Church, yet are worth reading by all.

Mary Howitt's Tales (2).

VII. AMERICAN WORKS OF FICTION.

Brown, Charles Brockden. Wieland, and Ormond (2),

Are American productions of great energy, but of a grave character.—*Kent.*

The Novels and Tales of J. Fenimore Cooper (1).

Mr. Cooper is too well known to American readers to require a favorable recommendation to them. His "Leather Stocking" Tales, and tales of the sea, are worthy of the highest place in the ranks of fiction.

Irving, Washington. Works (1).

His stories of "Rip Van Winkle," and the Legend of "Sleepy Hollow," are perhaps the finest pieces of original fictitious writing that this century has produced, next to the works of Scott.—*Chambers.*

Kennedy, John P. The Swallow-Barn (1).

An admirable delineation of Virginia life in the olden time. Another work by the same author, "Horse Shoe Robinson" (1), is of quite as much merit. Mr. Kennedy deserves a place in the front rank of American literature.—*Ch. King.*

Hawthorne, Nathaniel. The Scarlet Letter. The House of the Seven Gables, Twice Told Tales, &c. (1).

The author of these sterling works of genius deserves especial notice at the hands of Americans. There are few works of fiction of the present day, that exhibit so much originality, quaintness, and quiet humor, and are so full of thought. "The Scarlet Letter" deserves especial mention.

Paulding, James K. Dutchman's Fireside. Merry Tales, &c. (2).

Sedgwick, Catharine M. Hope Leslie; Redwood; and other Novels (1).

Works which have acquired for their author a distinguished reputation both at home and abroad.

Fay, Theo. S. Countess Ida. Norman Leslie (2).

Hoffman, Chas. Fenno. Greyslaer (2).

Judd, Sylvester. Margaret—a Tale of the Real and Ideal (2).

A work of great originality, not altogether free from blemishes of style, but still graceful and powerful.

Kirkland, Mrs. C. M. New Home. Forest Life (2).

Unequalled as pictures of Western life and manners, and written with a great deal of humor.

Longfellow, Henry W. Hyperion (1).

The production of a man of taste, refinement, and feeling; in truth, a pure poem.

Mitchell, Donald G. (*Ik Marvel*). *Reveries of a Bachelor, and Dream Life* (2).

An author who possesses a singular felicity of style, and who writes with much pathos, though deficient sometimes in power and boldness.

Poe, Edgar A. Tales (2).

McIntosh, Miss.

A writer of considerable power and force. "Two Lives," "Conquest and Self-Conquest," "Charms and Countercharms," &c., are from her pen.

Warner, Miss. Wide, Wide World. Queechy.

VIII.

GAMES, SPORTS, AND AMUSEMENTS.

Philidor's Analysis of Chess.

Staunton's Chess Player's Companion.

Chess Player's Hand-Book.

Stanley. American Chess Magazine.

Angell. Chess for Winter Evenings.

Kenny's Manual of Chess for Beginners.

A few standard works upon this most philosophical of games, were deemed worthy of a place in this volume.

Herbert, H. W. (Frank Forrester). Field Sporting in the United States and British North America.

—— —— Fish and Fishing of the United States and Canada.—Ch. King.

Whyte. History of British Turf.

Hofland. British Angler's Manual.

Carleton, J. W. Sporting Sketch Book.

Walker, Donald. Manly Exercises.

Herschberger. The Horseman.

Frost, Jno. Art of Swimming.

Strutts. Sports and Pastimes of the People of England.

Not without attraction to the descendants of those who engaged in these wild sports, now greatly modified, if not entirely effaced by time.

IX.

POLITICAL SCIENCE.

Carlyle on Chartism.

London Labor and the London Poor.
By the Brothers Mayhew.

The terrible irregularities in the social system of the Old World (from which we are not wholly exempt), are portrayed in these publications, which cannot be studied without impressing upon every healthy mind a sense of the duty of seeking some remedy for so great and dangerous ills.—*Ch. King.*

Wheaton, Henry. Elements of International Law (1).
Ch. King.

Dixon, Hepworth. John Howard and the Prison World of Europe.

MacPherson's Annals of Commerce (3).
Kent.

MacCulloch's Treatise on Commerce (2).
Kent.

Milton's Prose Works.

Written in the pure old English undefiled, and in the spirit of liberty.—*Ch. King.*

Fisher Ames's Works.
Kent.

Webster's Speeches.
Kent.

E. Everett's Speeches.
Kent.

Hazlitt. Political Essays.

Junius. Essays of.
Woodfall's edition.

CONSTITUTIONAL AND COMMERCIAL LAW.

Story's Conflict of Laws (1).
Ch. King.

W. A. Duer's Outlines of Constitutional Jurisprudence.
Ch. King.

Alfred Conkling. Young Citizen's Manual.
Ch. King.
It is a small work, which every young American should possess and study.

Jno. Duer on Insurance.

Starkie on Slander (1).
With Notes and References to American Cases, by John L. Wendell, Counsellor at Law.

The admirable preliminary essay of Judge Duer's noble treatise on the History and Objects of Insurance, is so distinguished by scholarly research, pure beauty of style, and legal acumen, as to render it attractive as well as useful to men in any way conversant with commercial affairs.

So again of the preliminary discourse of Starkie, extending through 70 pages, is of a character to interest and instruct all men; while the application of the law to American cases, by the present editor, gives additional value to the work. These two books are here commended to attention, let it be borne in mind, not to encourage commercial, or any other men, to be their own lawyers in disputed cases, than which few mistakes are more mischievous, but because its knowledge of general principles, so well imparted in those treatises, is always advantageous and ornamental to men in whatever business concerned.—*Ch. King.*

The Federalist (1).
By Hamilton Madison, and Jay, in 1 vol., 8vo. (1).

This is the best treatise that ever was written on republican government—the most true, the most instructive, and the most monitory. It is the most instructive book that ever was written on the necessity and value of the union of the States; and on the cherished hope entertained by those immortal patriots, that it might break and control the violence of faction—the mortal disease under which popular governments have everywhere perished.—*Kent.*

Story's Commentaries on the Constitution of the United States (1).

Just and true.—*Kent.*

De Tocqueville's Democracy in America (1).

It is a work of profound observation, and contains most wholesome admonition.—*Kent.*

Azuni's Maritime Law of Europe.
Kent.

Abbott on Shipping, Story's Edition.

Commercial Code of France.

Kent's Commentaries on American Law (1).
Eminently deserving the attention of every American.

X.

MORAL SCIENCE.

Paley's Moral Philosophy (2).
Kent.

Paley's Horæ Paulinæ (1).

Wayland's Elements of Moral Science (1).
Kent.

Mackintosh on the Progress of Ethical Philosophy (1).
Kent.

The first named treatise loses none of its value by comparison with the more modern and elaborate Bridgewater treatises. In the last named, is a most satisfactory and conclusive demonstration from internal evidence alone, of the authenticity of Paul's epistles.

Brown's Philosophy of the Human Mind (1).
Kent.

Abercrombie on the Moral Feelings (2).
Kent.

Dr. Lieber's Political Ethics (1).
Kent.

Adams, Jno. Q. Letters to his Son, on the Bible (2).

Butler. Analogy of Natural and Revealed Religion (1).
Ch. King.

The Bridgewater Treatises (1).

These are eight in number, and those of Dr. Buckland, and the Rev. Mr. Whewell, already mentioned, take the first rank.—*Kent.*

Verplanck on the Evidences of Christianity (1).
Kent.

Watson's Apology for Christianity (1).
Kent.

Watson's Apology for the Bible (1).
Kent.

Lardner's Credibility of the Gospel History (2).
Kent.

Newton on the Prophecies (1).
Kent.

Dr. Spring on the Obligations of the World to the Bible (1).
Kent.

Morrell's Philosophy of Religion (2).

Adams, Rev. Mr. The Elements of Christian Science (1).

An American treatise of high excellence and original views, forcibly inculcated.—*Ch. King.*

Sauch. Light of Nature (2).

A work characterized by Robert Hall as one in which the noblest philosophy is brought down by a master hand, and placed within the reach of every man of sound understanding.—*Ch. King.*

Foster's Essays (1).

Sound religion and fervid genius, enlisted in the cause of man's government and instruction.—*Ch. King.*

Chalmers. Christianity Applied to Commerce (1).
Ch. King.

Dymond. Principles of Morality (2).
Ch. King.

——— *On War and Christianity* (2).
Ch. King.

Tayler Lewis. Plato against the Atheists (1).
Ch. King.

Cousin's Elements of Psychology (2).
From the French.—*Ch. King.*

Tupper's Proverbial Philosophy (2).
Ch. King.

Upham, Thos. C. Life of Mdl. de la Motte Guyon, with some account of the Opinions and Life of Fenelon, Archbishop of Cambray (2).

A valuable unfolding of character, and of the influence of religious opinions and associations, even amid the gayeties and temptations of a brilliant French life.—*Ch. King.*

Cousin, Victor. Introduction to History of Philosophy (2).
Ch. King.

Feltham, Owen. Resolves—Divine and Moral (1).
Ch. King.

XI.

NATURAL SCIENCES.

I. NATURAL PHILOSOPHY, CHEMISTRY, GEOLOGY, AND MINERALOGY, Etc.

Humboldt. Cosmos (1).
Translated by E. Sabine.

——— *Aspects of Nature.*

These admirable works have commanded much attention from scientific men, and are worthy of their renowned author.

Guyot. Earth and Man (1).
From the French.—*Ch. King.*

Pritchard. Physical History of Man (1).
Ch. King.

Somerville, Mrs. Physical Geography (1).
Ch. King.

Mantell's Medals of Creation (1).

From a very competent hand, and calculated to awaken interest.—*Bp. Potter.*

Chalmers, Thomas. Adaptation of Nature to Man (1).
(Bridgewater Treatise.)—*Ch. King.*

Anderson, Jno., D. D. Course of Creation (2).

A work, the result of long years of labor, thought, and universal travel. It requires close study and large acquirements, to be apprehended in all its vast and varied topics.—*Ch. King.*

Beckman's History of Inventions (2).
Ch. King.

Ewbank's Hydraulics (2).

A work of extraordinary research, and much curious and rare information.—*Ch. King.*

Quekett on the Use of the Microscope (1).

Liebig's Animal Chemistry (1).

——— *Familiar Letters on Chemistry.*

Draper, Jno. W. Text-Book on Chemistry (1).

Farraday. Researches and Experiments in Electricity (1).

Bakewell's Introduction to Geology (2).
Kent.

Lyell's Geology (2).
Kent.

Miller, Hugh. First Impressions of England and its People (2).

——— ——— *Old Red Sandstone; or, New Walks in an Old Field* (1).

——— ——— *Footprints of the Creator* (1).

These are remarkable works of a remarkable man—(a stone quarrier in Scotland)—whose fervent and observing mind, and reverent, yet bold and inquiring spirit, and admirable self-culture under adverse circumstances, have raised him to the highest rank among Geologists and eloquent writers. The last work on the list, though a book of travels, and marred, as to subjects of church, and church government, and church edifices, with much prejudice, is yet a treatise on Geology, and very well executed.—*Ch. King.*

Hitchcock, Edward, LL. D., (Pres. of Amherst College), Religion of Geology, and its Connected Sciences (1).

A work eminent for candor, science, and learning, which reconciles seeming difficulties, and adds to the general character of the subject discussed, by great force and beauty of style.—*Ch. King.*

Cuvier's Theory of the Earth (2).
Kent.

Professor Olmsted on Natural Philosophy (1).
Kent.

Professor Olmsted on Astronomy (1).
Kent.

Herschel's Treatise on Natural Philosophy (1).
Kent.

Bourne, Ed. Catechism of the Steam Engine (1).

Treatise on the Steam Engine (1).
By the Artisan Club.

Renwick on the Steam Engine (2).
Kent.

Brewster, Sir David. Letters on Natural Magic (1).

Somerville, Mrs. Connection of the Physical Sciences (1).

Babbage, C. Ninth Bridgewater Treatise (1).

Mill's System of Logic (1).

Logic and Utility of Mathematics (1).
By CHARLES DAVIES, LL. D.

These two works are classed together, rather because of the one connecting link of logic, of which mathematical reasoning is the severed form, than from any general similarity of topics or treatment. Yet the reason which will master Mill, will relish more exceedingly the admirable work of Prof. Davies, which should be attentively read, and may be readily apprehended by intelligent minds, although unimbued with science.—*Ch. King.*

Carpenter, W. B. Human Physiology and Physiological Anatomy.

Macnish, Robert. Anatomy of Drunkenness.

——— ——— *Philosophy of Sleep.*

Grant, Robert E. Outlines of Comparative Anatomy.

Owen on Comparative Anatomy.

These works have entirely superseded the work of Cuvier, and are not only much more reliable, but are full of new and interesting information.

II. NATURAL HISTORY.

Buffon. Natural History (2).
Kent.

Goldsmith, O. Animated Nature (2).
Kent.

Ord's Life of Wilson (2).

Wilson's Ornithology (1).

The first of these narratives, the life of our first American Ornithologist; the second is his own history of our own Birds; their habits, manners, and almost language, written with a rare enthusiasm and love, and intelligence of nature.—*Ch. King.*

Sir Wm. Jardine's Various Treatises in the Naturalist's Library, on Animals and Birds (1).—*Ch. King.*

Huber on Bees (1).

Jos. Taylor on the Dog (2).

White. Natural History of Selborne (1).

Kirby and Spence. Introduction to Entomology (1).

All charming works, and amid the busy life of a metropolis, refreshing.—*Ch. King.*

Kirby, Wm. History, Habits, &c., of Animals (1).
(Bridgewater Treatise.)

Mudie's British Naturalist (1).

Episodes of Insect Life (1).

One of the most delightful works upon this truly interesting branch of Natural History that has ever been published. We commend it to the especial attention of the reader.

Audubon. Birds of America (1).

——— *Quadrupeds of America* (1).

Works that are a noble monument to the energy and perseverance of their distinguished author.

Howitt's Book of the Seasons (1).

Hunt, Robert. Poetry of Science (2).

Gardiner's Music of Nature (2).

An attempt to prove, by many interesting illustrations, that what is impassioned and pleasing in singing, instrumental music, and speech, is derived from the sounds of animated nature.—*Ch. King.*

Harris on the Insects of Massachusetts (3).

Brockleby, John. Views of the Microscopic World (1).

Cooper, Miss. Rural Hours (1).

III. ASTRONOMY.

Herschel. Treatise on Astronomy (1).

Olmsted, Denison. Introduction to Astronomy (1).

Whewell, Wm. Astronomy and Physics in reference to Natural Theology.—(Bridgewater Treatise.)

Nichol. Architecture of the Heavens (1).

The Planetary and Stellar Worlds (1).
By O. M. Mitchell.

These are two noble treatises on the most sublime of studies, Astronomy, and are attractive and intelligible alike to the learned and unlearned.—*Ch. King.*

Nichol, J. P. The Stellar Universe (1).

Nichol, J. P. Thoughts on the System of the World (1).

Both excellent treatises upon these attractive subjects.

Dick, Thos. The Sidereal Heavens (2).

The sidereal heavens, and other subjects connected with Astronomy, are depicted as illustrative of the Deity, and of an infinity of worlds.

Blunt, Charles J. Beauty of the Heavens (2).

Hind's Solar System (1).

IV. BOTANY, GARDENING, Etc.

Loudon, Mrs. Various Botanical Works.
Ch. King.

Torrey and Gray. Flora of North America (3).
Ch. King.

The North American Sylva.
By Michaux, with Continuation by Nuttall. In all, 6 vols.

A complete history of our American forest trees, with fine plates, so well executed and colored, as to enable every one to become acquainted with, and to discriminate between the varieties of trees.—*Ch. King.*

Downing. Fruits and Fruit Trees of America.

——— *Landscape Gardening, and Rural Architecture.*

By these admirable works, Mr. Downing has done much to improve the taste of our rural inhabitants, and at the same time to promote the best and most judicious selection and culture of Fruit Trees. It is one of the most common and earnest longings of the toiling residents of cities, to be able one day to return to a snuggery in the country; and these admirable works will both minister to these longings, and teach how to realize them satisfactorily. —*Ch. King.*

Gray's Genera of the Plants of North America (2).

——— *Botanical Text-Book* (1).

www.ingramcontent.com/pod-product-compliance
Lightning Source LLC
LaVergne TN
LVHW021419110826
845150LV00007B/1999

9781425509385